THE CLARKSON GORDON STORY

1864–1989

DAVID MacKENZIE

The
Clarkson Gordon
Story

IN CELEBRATION OF 125 YEARS

CLARKSON GORDON

Printed in Canada by University of Toronto Press

ISBN 0-9691100-2-2

Canadian Cataloguing in Publication Data
MacKenzie, David Clark, 1953–
  The Clarkson Gordon story
  ISBN 0-969110-02-2
  1. Clarkson, Gordon & Co. – History.
  I. Clarkson, Gordon (Firm). II. Title.
  HF5616.C23C43 1989   338.7'61657'0971   C89-093399-5

1864 · 1989
CLARKSON GORDON

Committed to the future,
indebted to our past

Contents

Foreword

THE CELEBRATION of our 125th anniversary gives us a chance to pause and reflect – an opportunity to look back over the years with pride and satisfaction. Clarkson Gordon traces its origins back to 1864 and Thomas Clarkson's small Toronto-based trustee and receivership business. From this modest beginning Clarkson Gordon has evolved into a leading Canadian professional firm, offering a diversity of services in accounting, auditing, taxation, consulting and insolvency. Today we operate in both official languages from coast to coast in Canada, and throughout the world as a major partner of Arthur Young International. Our clients range from small family businesses to some of the largest multinational corporations.

This history is a record of that astounding growth and a chronicle of the people who have made Clarkson Gordon the success that it is today. It is our way of honouring past achievements and of acknowledging the value and uniqueness of our inheritance. It is also recognition that our achievements of tomorrow will be built on the foundations of our past.

Clarkson Gordon is proud to have been able to serve Canadians for 125 years. Looking ahead, we welcome the challenges and opportunities of the future, confident in our determination and ability to continue providing superior service to our clients in Canada and around the world.

William A. Farlinger, Chairman
September 1988

Acknowledgements

THIS BOOK WAS UNDERTAKEN as part of Clarkson Gordon's 125th anniversary celebrations. During the researching and writing of this history, I received the utmost co-operation and assistance from many individuals. My thanks go to Douglas Dolan, who helped me in a number of ways, as researcher, interviewer and editor.

I would especially like to thank A.J. Little for his kind permission to make free use of his original text, written for the firm's 100th anniversary in 1964, which forms much of the first third of this book. "It was for him a labour of love," J.R.M. Wilson wrote in 1964, "but we know that it also proved to be both time consuming and demanding. We are all very grateful for the effort and the result."

Finally, I would like to thank all the senior executives and retired partners who graciously gave of their time and answered all of our questions candidly. Without their co-operation, this history could not have been written.

David MacKenzie

David MacKenzie
September 1988

THE CLARKSON GORDON STORY
1864–1989

CHAPTER ONE

A Snapshot
of the Firm Today

"COMMITTED TO THE FUTURE, indebted to our past." In 1986, the partners of Clarkson Gordon and Woods Gordon met to consider and discuss the future directions of the firm and what, if any, of the strengths of the past needed modification to meet the challenges of the future. Nowhere was the process better described than in the motto developed for the celebration of the firm's 125th anniversary in 1989. Not that the partners had not spoken before, of course – often, strongly and independently. This time there was a major difference. The firm was building a new strategic plan, a summing-up of the best from the past and the almost endless possibilities for the future. A responsive chord had been struck, and it seemed that everyone wanted to express his or her deepest feelings and aspirations. During the following year, consultation and discussion continued in every office across Canada and the plan took shape.

Having a plan is only the beginning. Executing the plan is what counts. With the plan completed, the dialogue still goes on, as the 3,300 people of the firm implement the initiatives that combine the best of personal and professional commitments, within the huge and complex fabric of Canadian business.

As partnerships, Clarkson Gordon and Woods Gordon currently represent almost 420 partners and, through them, a broader constituency of almost 2,100 other professionals and some 800 administrative and general support staff. Clarkson Gordon, as a public accounting practice, can admit only chartered accountants to partnership. It has 358 partners. Woods Gordon, the management consulting practice, has partners with a broad range of professional backgrounds. In addition, all Clarkson Gordon partners are also partners of Woods Gordon. As well, a number of Clarkson Gordon partners and staff members are employed in the trustee and receivership practice, Clarkson Gordon Inc. This interweaving of people and practices allows the best of service to clients, and, taken together, they are known as "The Firm".

Response to clients' needs with high-quality service has been the basis of the firm's practice, and the ability to both anticipate and respond to an enormous range of such needs has built the partnership into a substantial business in its own right. The firm is national – "home-grown" and proud of it, with twenty-six offices from St. John's, Newfoundland to Victoria, British Columbia. It is also multinational, both through its own investment in other countries and through its membership in Arthur Young International. With more than 20,000 Canadian clients and revenues approaching a quarter of a billion dollars a year, the firm has far more than a theoretical knowledge of business. It both gives good advice and follows its own advice. It best understands the business world by being an energetic and competitive business itself, while never losing sight of the professional and ethical foundation on which it is built.

Like all businesses, Clarkson Gordon and Woods Gordon operate in an increasingly complex environment. The firm's Executive Committee (equivalent to a Board of Directors) and Operations Policy Committee (equivalent to a day-to-day senior management) meet frequently and direct the firm's activities through the medium of the Office Managing Partners.

Intensive analysis of significant environmental factors is a major part of the strategic planning process, and the firm's cross-Canada review in 1986 and 1987 identified many issues that the firm, along with the rest of the business world, had to address. They included continued regional disparities, the anticipation of relatively modest real growth in the economy, the continued importance of international trade, the concentration of pools of

4

capital, ever-present and ongoing tax reform, and government policy that would continue to encourage the formation of small and start-up businesses. In many cases, the firm had created or strengthened practice areas to be ready to assist clients in dealing with such environmental trends.

Competition is one of the areas where the public accounting world has changed in the 1980s. The firm's competition is both strong and good. That merely sets the challenge to stay on top. Marketing − not a natural strength of most who seek to become chartered accountants − has become much more aggressive, in terms both of acquiring and retaining clients and of seeking the best possible candidates for the profession in order to develop high-performing professionals. Clients' expectations have also increased, in both the depth and the range of services, and the firm has responded with such strategies as major investment in industry specialization, expanded educational programs, and growth in size.

Vigorous competition, in a subtle way, reflects one of the best things about the culture of the firm. Many competitors are people the firm has trained, and, like the people who have stayed, their quality represents stringent policies aimed at hiring and developing high-performance people. There is an extension of that part of the firm's culture. The nature of the profession is such that only about one in ten of those who join will eventually enter the partnership. For the others it is a "hands-on" introduction to the world of business, and many go on to make vital contributions to that "fabric." The firm takes great pride in the contribution of its partners and in the contribution to Canadian business of its "old boys − and girls".

In their numbers and in their range of talents, the alumni participate in diverse ways across Canada. Of the more than 5,000 in total, more than 200 alumni are company presidents; some 750 are in senior financial or other roles as vice-presidents and directors; over 400 are senior practitioners; and almost 100 are post-secondary business educators. There is particular satisfaction with the latter fact. The firm has always exhibited strong leadership both in research and development and in education, whether within the firm or in support of the nation's universities. It is the point where the firm's commitment to the future begins.

Neither the past nor the future has ever been forgotten at the firm. Tradition and opportunity coexist, and shape each other. The time was right in 1986 for the reconsideration of the existing, and development of a new, consultation-based strategic plan.

Consider the management demands, given the growth and diversity of the firm: more than four hundred partners, characterized by one senior partner as "rugged individualists", spread out over more than four thousand miles, all with major but differing client and professional responsibilities. Supporting them are thousands more of the same type of high-performing people. The only real asset of the firm was the intellect, experience and commitment of those who considered themselves part of it. Every partner ran his or her own business, and yet all were part of one business. What held them together? What did they have in common, and had it changed over the years? After all, as the firm was getting bigger, it was getting "younger". Almost half the present partners are forty or younger; almost three-quarters have been partners for ten years or less. Were the old values holding?

Strategic plans had always been developed for the firm, so the idea was not new. But there was something about the 1986 plan, and the readiness of the partners, that created a groundswell of involvement, a testing of personal values and goals against those of the firm.

New elements of the strategic planning process were introduced in 1986. Values were probed, consensual discussion groups got together, revisions met with responses, and a contemporary version of the firm's mission was developed as the expression of the common cause of the organization and its stakeholders. The wording changed from that of the preceding mission statement, but only to reflect the current environment. None of the underlying values changed, although many were amplified. The partners reaffirmed their commitment to the traditional values on which the firm had built its reputation, to the provision of superior service to clients and to their shared values and responsibilities to each other.

The mission statement can never be achieved. It is like a North Star, a simple and enduring navigational guide. It provides direction, and from it flow the strategies, tactics and actions that become the full plan in the day-to-day world of implementation. The whole process requires careful crafting, repetition and review.

In terms of time, this chapter deals with the present. It is a summing-up and description of the nature and challenges of the partnership. It is a base from which the three parts of the mission statement can be examined to see how well the earlier questions, such as "what held the firm together?", and "what did the partners have in common?" are answered. It is a confirmation of the continuing and underlying values of the firm.

The Firm's mission is to be the leading, most respected and successful public accounting and management consulting firm in Canada.

One of the most significant partnership values identified by the partners during the planning process was "pride in self and firm". The firm has been a leader in both public accounting and management consulting throughout its history, and that was reflected in an informed and quiet pride. Not a sense of pride out of touch with reality, nor one that "goeth before a fall". Rather, the pride of being associated with predecessors and colleagues of the highest standards of ethics and competence, and the recognition of the vigilance required to ensure that every action taken on behalf of the firm and its clients would continue to meet these demanding standards. Leadership had taken many forms, within the firm, the profession, the business community, and the government. Leadership continues to flourish in terms of innovative business advice, increased size and range of services, technical research and development and the development of professional staff.

7

We are committed to unsurpassed personal service to our clients and to maintaining the public trust by achieving the highest professional standards of competence, independence and objectivity in all our opinions and advice.

The firm is a service organization. Its *raison d'être*, and societal value, are to help organizations be robust and enduring, within the needs and expectations of the public at large. The stakeholder analysis done during the strategic planning process clearly identified both clients and the public as groups that had a vested interest in the performance of the firm and its people. These commitments were reflected in three of the most significant partnership values identified: "intensely personal client service", "understanding the client's business", and "unsurpassed personal and professional standards of competence, independence and objectivity".

The partners are keenly aware of the fine balance between the need for empathy with clients and the need for objectivity. They believe that they best serve the business community by knowing as much as possible about how their clients' organizations operate. The desired professional adviser is trusted and provides reliable information and objective, challenging advice. To excel in client service means to deliver a focused range of outstanding-quality professional services in minimum response time, through knowing the client's business and the environment in which it operates. To do so means that the firm has developed and maintained organizational patterns that maximize direct partner-client contact yet provide for consultation and review, so that partners bring to bear the talents of individuals with broad backgrounds and specialized knowledge, with appropriate cross-checks on technical quality and independence.

Independence is paramount, and the partners and staff take considerable measures to ensure that their business judgements and advice are made independently and objectively. A licence to practice is a public trust, and the firm supports the pursuit of strong self-regulation, both among its own and within the profession. A large number of firm policies and procedures exist to assist partners and staff in this regard. The policies and procedures are a back-up, not a substitute, for the individual's professional and ethical positions. In summary, the members of the firm behave both as good corporate citizens and as good citizens.

Our commitment embodies respect for our people and for our clients in the pursuit of excellence in all that we do.

The last of the five major values of the partnership articulated during the strategic planning process was "high personal performance expectations". In recruitment, development and rewards for performance, the firm has always set very high standards for its people. The challenges and risks inherent in public practice need intelligent, innovative, practical and tough-minded people who have the ability to make decisions and the confidence to stand behind them. The firm has always sought, and found, such people.

A significant part of the firm's culture is to show respect for successful people by continually challenging them and increasing their responsibilities at the earliest opportunity. Although financial reward has always been an important part of the picture, the firm is well aware that it is often a surrogate for recognition of the contribution made. The driving incentive for the kind of people that the firm wants – and has – will be the opportunity for growth and responsibility in the workplace.

When the partners began talking among themselves during the strategic planning process, the intensity and extent of involvement were surprising. As the plan continues to unfold, it is a surprise no longer. The old values have held, have been internalized and continue to shape and direct the actions of the firm's people. A belief in competence, superior service and the highest personal standards has flowed from the earliest day forward. As leaders of the firm have followed their predecessors, one by one, they have demonstrated by personal action what these beliefs meant, and their partners understand and behave on the basis of the same intrinsic values.

At first glance, the surveys and consensus-seeking activities during the development of the new strategic plan showed remarkable consistency of values and priorities across the country and the partnership. On reflection, it was not the consistency that was remarkable: it was the strength and influence of the people who guided and developed the firm throughout its history, instilling fundamental values and acting as their steward for succeeding generations.

Now we can reach back to the beginnings of the firm to try to understand the nature of those who built it, and how they did so. Thomas Clarkson was the first ...

CHAPTER TWO

Thomas Clarkson
and the Origins of the Firm

I N 1864, THOMAS CLARKSON, then aged
sixty-two, returned to Toronto from Milwaukee, Wisconsin,
where he had spent the previous four years establishing a grain
brokerage business with his sons. On moving back to Canada, he
resumed his earlier career as a commission agent and wholesale
dealer in grain and stocks; he also acted as an insurance agent,
conducting his affairs from an office on Front Street.

Already a prominent and respected member of the Toronto
business community, Thomas Clarkson, in that same year, was
appointed an Official Assignee by the Province of Canada. In this
new capacity he began developing the trustee and receivership
business that would ultimately evolve into an independent
accounting practice. It is from 1864, therefore, that the present
firm dates its beginnings.

II

Thomas Clarkson was born in Sussworth, in the English county of
Lincolnshire, on January 26, 1802. At the age of thirty he
emigrated to Upper Canada and settled in York, then a small town
of about eight thousand people.

Upper Canada in the 1830s was still a separate colony within
British North America. When the Act of Union (proclaimed in
1841) created the united Province of Canada, that part formerly
called Upper Canada was designated Canada West, although the

name apparently had no legal status. The town of York, meanwhile, was incorporated as a city in 1834 and renamed Toronto.

Thomas Clarkson had been married in England, but his first wife died in 1829 before he came to Canada. He married again two years after his arrival in the colony; his second wife also died very early in life – although not before adding four more children to the pair born of his first marriage in England. A third marriage followed, on May 2, 1844, at St. James' Cathedral in Toronto; the bride was Sarah Helliwell, daughter of a well-known Toronto family. Of the ten children produced by this union, it was the fifth, Edward Roper Curzon Clarkson, who would later carry on the family business.

In the early years, Thomas Clarkson was a retail merchant; he subsequently operated an auctioneering business and about 1850 established a produce and commission business on Front Street, evidently specializing in the grain trade. Records of his activity from 1832 to 1860 are incomplete, but a reference in the Toronto Commercial Directory for 1836–7 lists him as a storekeeper at 55 Yonge Street. This is confirmed by information contained in *The Windmill*, an account of the early days of Messrs. Gooderham and Worts; a listing of their principal customers in 1838 includes "Thomas Clarkson & Co., general storekeeper, 55 Yonge Street, on ground now occupied by the R. Simpson Co." Later in the same history, in a section dealing with business conditions and sales volume for 1840, there is the following reference to the store:

"Best" whiskey brought 2s. 6d. by the barrel and was in better demand – the sales amounting to nearly 1300 gallons, of which Thomas Clarkson & Co. took nearly 850. It will be remembered that this shop was at the Yonge Street corner of Macaulay Town and the demand for a better quality here possibly indicated an improvement in the residential character of the western and northern districts.

In the 1830s, "Macaulay Town" was the area on the north side of Queen Street (then called Lot Street) from Yonge Street west to Osgoode Hall. Thomas Clarkson's store seems to have been located

Thomas Clarkson

at the southwest corner of Yonge and Queen streets – in 1869, the first location of Timothy Eaton's famous department store (and later the site of the rival Robert Simpson Company).

From 1850 until he moved to the United States a decade later, Thomas Clarkson was a leading member of the Toronto business community. As his various enterprises prospered, he found time to take an active role in other aspects of the city's commercial life as well as in community affairs. He was President of the Commercial Building & Investment Society, a successful venture incorporated in 1851 and patterned after the building societies formed in England to finance housing construction. He was also one of the

13

promoters of the Toronto and Georgian Bay Canal Company. In 1852 he became the second President of the Toronto Board of Trade, which he had helped to found; in 1856, he became a member of the new Bank of Toronto's first Board of Directors.

The establishment, in 1860, of the Milwaukee grain brokerage Thomas Clarkson & Sons brought Benjamin Reid Clarkson and Robert Guy Clarkson into partnership with their father. In Thomas Clarkson's absence, the Toronto business was carried on by the firm Clarkson, Hunter & Co. When Thomas Clarkson returned to Canada in 1864, he resumed a direct role in his prospering Toronto enterprises and at the same time launched a venture that, in retrospect, is seen as the origin of the modern firm.

The year 1864 was a crucial one in the history of Canada. For some time, the Maritime provinces had been considering the possibility of confederation and were planning a conference to discuss the matter. The far-sighted John A. Macdonald was thinking along similar lines for the whole of British North America and persuaded the Maritime governments to invite representatives of the Province of Canada to attend as well. The conference was held in Charlottetown in September 1864. This meeting led to certain general areas of agreement and was followed by the Quebec Conference in October of the same year. From that point, three of the four provinces (Prince Edward Island remaining aloof) moved slowly but steadily toward the Confederation of 1867, which saw the Province of Canada divided into two provinces, Ontario and Quebec, and joined with Nova Scotia and New Brunswick to form the Dominion of Canada.

By 1864, business conditions in Canada had not been good for several years. Trade with the United States was seriously disrupted by the American Civil War, which had broken out in 1861 and was to continue through most of 1865 (Abraham Lincoln was shot on April 14 of that year). In addition, successive droughts and infestations of insects had resulted in poor harvests for three years running. In spite of these adverse conditions, or perhaps because of them, Thomas Clarkson's enterprises flourished, particularly the trustee business.

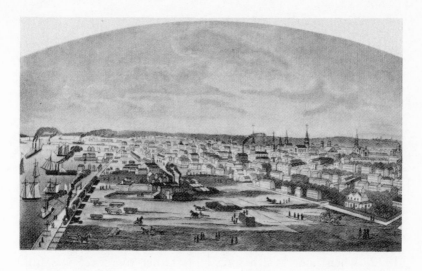

Toronto, 1864

By this time, Toronto had become a thriving financial centre. The population had grown to 48,000, about six times what it had been when Thomas Clarkson first arrived in 1832. Transportation links to the rest of the continent were good, with the Grand Trunk, Great Western and Northern railways all running into the first Union Station, at the foot of York Street. Public transport within the city was also much improved; the Toronto Street Railway Company, formed in 1861, enjoyed a franchise to operate horse-drawn vehicles and by December of that year boasted eleven cars, a number of sleighs and wagons, seventy horses and six miles of track. The city streets, as well as many houses and places of business, were lit by gas supplied by the Consumers Gas Company (incorporated in 1848).

Early in 1870, Thomas Clarkson's son, E.R.C. Clarkson (who had been working in Montreal), moved back to Toronto to join the family firm. Thomas Clarkson was forced to retire because of ill health in 1872, leaving the trustee and bankruptcy business in the hands of his son and Thomas Munro. On May 4, 1874, Thomas Clarkson died in Toronto at the age of seventy-two. He was buried in St. James's Cemetery.

Edward Roper Curzon Clarkson, known as "E.R.C." to friends and associates, was born on August 11, 1852, in his father's home at 278 King Street East, Toronto. Soon after his twelfth birthday he was enrolled in Upper Canada College, then located at the corner of King and Simcoe streets. Upon graduation in June 1867, he was sent by his father to Montreal to gain some mercantile experience. The firm Lewis, Kay & Co., dealers in wholesale dry goods, employed him at a salary of £25 per annum. In 1870, when he returned to Toronto at his father's request to help run the family business, he was just seventeen years old.

E.R.C. Clarkson devoted all of his time to trustee work and, by 1872, when poor health forced his father to retire, was fully conversant with that side of the business and quite prepared to take over. Unfortunately, he was still under twenty-one and therefore not eligible to receive the appointment as an official assignee of the province. The appointment went instead to his employee, Thomas Munro, and a new partnership was formed. The firm Clarkson and Munro carried on the business from 1872 until 1877, at which point E.R.C. Clarkson received his government appointment. He then joined a Mr. Turner in the firm Turner, Clarkson & Co. That partnership continued until 1881, when E.R.C. Clarkson went into business under his name alone.

During this time, E.R.C. Clarkson became increasingly interested in the practice of accountancy, and in November 1879 he was one of twelve sponsors who called a special meeting of accountants to discuss the establishment of a professional society. There were no chartered accountants in Canada at this time. The earliest formal accounting society had been founded twenty-five years earlier in Scotland, when a group of Edinburgh accountants formed a voluntary association and was granted a royal charter. Since that landmark inauguration of "The Society of Accountants in Edinburgh" in 1854, many similar organizations had been established in Great Britain.

The Toronto meeting resulted in the formation of an unincorporated society, the Institute of Accountants and Adjusters of

E.R.C. Clarkson

Canada, in December 1879; E.R.C. Clarkson was elected to the
first nine-member council and joined in petitioning for the charter
of an Ontario institute. In 1883, the Institute of Chartered
Accountants of Ontario was incorporated by a special act of the
legislature. Soon thereafter, E.R.C. Clarkson presented himself
for examination before the Institute Council so that he would be
entitled to use the designation "Chartered Accountant". He later
became President of the Institute, which claimed to be the first
such body in the country. (The Association of Accountants in
Montreal held an initial meeting just a few days after its Ontario
counterpart, in December 1879, and the following year became
the first such society in Canada to be incorporated. It has since

evolved, through several name changes, into l'Ordre des comptables agréés du Québec.)

IV

E.R.C. Clarkson conducted business in his own name until 1891, when he formed the partnership Clarkson & Cross, which also handled trustee and bankruptcy work. W.H. Cross, born in Manchester in 1845, had been engaged by Mr. Clarkson in 1890 to assist in the accounting practice. He had trained as an accountant in England before coming to Canada, where he settled first in Hamilton and later in Toronto. A brilliant man and a genius with figures, he was one of the founders of the Ontario Institute.

The firm's financial record for 1890 gives a good indication of the scale of the accounting practice in those years:

Fees earned		$6,947
Unpaid	$2,800	
Uncharged	480	
		3,280
		$3,667
Expenses		1,674
		$1,993
Drawn by W.H. Cross		2,115
Advanced by E.R.C. Clarkson		$ 122

E.R.C. Clarkson, like his father, had a very large family – seven sons and five daughters. Three of his sons joined him in the business: Geoffrey Teignmouth in 1893, at age fifteen, Frederick Curzon in 1896, at age sixteen, and Guy in 1906, at age eighteen. Of the three, only Geoffrey sat the accountancy examination; he was active in both the trustee work and the accountancy practice.

In this early period, one of the accounting students articled to W.H. Cross was John F. Helliwell, a relative of E.R.C. Clarkson (whose mother was Sarah Helliwell). In 1897, John Helliwell went to Vancouver to establish the firm Clarkson, Cross & Helliwell. Unfortunately, because of the great distance and inadequate communications between Toronto and the west coast, neither firm contributed much to the other, and by mutual agreement the association was terminated in 1910. John Helliwell continued in practice in Vancouver; the successful firm he founded, Helliwell, Maclachlan & Co., later merged with Thorne, Riddell (now Thorne Ernst & Whinney).

E.R.C. Clarkson had a distinguished reputation in the business community, and his advice and counsel were particularly sought by financial institutions. He was able to wind up insolvent businesses quickly and realize cash for the creditors. However, he did not think this policy was good for the banks and other large creditors, or indeed for the country as a whole. He finally persuaded one of the banks to let him manage a company that was in difficulty, instead of winding it up. His success in guiding the enterprise out of trouble was vitally important to the small community where it was located and, at the same time, saved a profitable client for the bank. This concern for getting companies back on track rather than presiding over their demise was to become a hallmark of the firm's philosophy in the years that followed, and remains so today.

As the firm grew, E.R.C. Clarkson maintained his involvement in the overall development of the profession. Early in 1902, a group of practising accountants, not all of them members of one of the provincial institutes, announced its intention of applying to the Dominion government for incorporation of a new Institute of Accounting. The institute would provide standardized education in accounting and allow its members to use the title "Chartered Accountant" anywhere in Canada. The new organization, the Dominion Association of Chartered Accountants, was incorporated on May 15, 1902, with E.R.C. Clarkson, W.H. Cross and John F. Helliwell (then with the Vancouver partnership) among the twenty petitioners.

For some years, the Dominion Association continued to admit members and permit them to use the designation "Chartered Accountant". The Ontario Institute, however, attempted to restrict the practice of chartered accountancy in that province to its own membership. Relations between the two bodies were less than cordial, but by the latter part of 1909 agreement was reached as to a future course for the profession in Canada. In 1910, amendments to the Dominion Association by-laws made it the co-ordinating body for the country. It then ceased to grant degrees, and its members were given the right to join provincial institutes. In 1951, the Dominion Association was renamed the Canadian Institute of Chartered Accountants.

V

The regard in which E.R.C. Clarkson was held in the business community is evident in the various appointments that distinguished the latter part of his career. He was elected a director of Canada Permanent Mortgage Corporation (now part of Canada Trustco Mortgage Company) in 1912, and ten years later became a Vice-President. In 1914, he assumed a directorship of The Manufacturers Life Insurance Company. He held these and other important posts until his death in 1931.

Finally, in addition to his achievements in the accounting practice and in the development of the profession as a whole, E.R.C. Clarkson's legacy to the present firm includes one other key element: the hiring, in 1898, of a young accountant named Harry Duncan Lockhart Gordon – but for that part of the story we must turn to a new chapter.

CHAPTER THREE

The Making
of the Partnership

Harry Duncan Lockhart Gordon
was born in Toronto on July 20, 1873, the eldest in a family of
five brothers (one of whom died in infancy) and three sisters. His
father, a lawyer, had emigrated to Canada from Scotland in 1868
and established a practice in Toronto. The family home was on
Windsor Street, a small street running north/south between
Wellington and Front, just west of John Street.

H.D.L. Gordon attended Upper Canada College, then went on
to the Royal Military College in Kingston, graduating in 1894.
He worked briefly keeping the books for a brokerage that dealt in
sterling exchange for the banks, but seeing little prospect for
advancement he decided instead to study for his C.A. degree. After
consulting with E.R.C. Clarkson, he went to England and found
employment with Messrs. Cooper Brothers & Co., a large firm of
accountants in London. In 1898, he passed the final examinations
of the Society of Incorporated Accountants and Auditors (an
English organization later merged with the Institute of Chartered
Accountants in England and Wales) and returned to Canada. That
same year he was granted a C.A. degree by the Ontario Institute.

Mr. Gordon joined the staff of Clarkson & Cross in 1898 and
remained with the firm for not quite eight years. In 1905 he
planned to get married, and as the firm had no partnership
opportunity available for him it was mutually agreed that he
might do better on his own. Following his marriage in February of
that year, he opened his own accounting practice. His first
assignment was to manage the newly incorporated Penny Bank,

which offered a system through which children could save their pennies and deposit them at school. The bank post, which he retained until 1913, provided him with office space, a stenographer and a small honorarium. Meanwhile, the accounting practice grew quickly, so that in less than a year it was necessary to find a competent assistant. The man engaged for this job was a graduate accountant named Robert James Dilworth.

Robert Dilworth was born in Trinity Square, Toronto, on February 13, 1869. His father, James Dilworth of Belfast, Ireland, had come to Canada as a soldier. After graduating from Dufferin Public School and Jarvis Collegiate in Toronto, Robert Dilworth worked for various employers – including Geoffrey T. Clarkson, eldest son of E.R.C. Clarkson – as office boy, bookkeeper and office manager. Perhaps because of his experience with the Clarkson firm, Robert Dilworth decided to study for an accounting degree and, at the age of thirty-two, articled to Messrs. Jenkins & Hardy. He obtained his C.A. degree in 1903.

Shortly thereafter, H.D.L. Gordon approached Robert Dilworth and offered him a position at an annual salary, with the understanding that he could develop business for his own account, provided it took no more than half of his time and on the condition that half of any fees he charged to his personal clients would be deducted from his salary. This arrangement proved satisfactory and profitable from the start, and one year later, on April 1, 1907, the two men formed the new firm Gordon & Dilworth. Under the first partnership agreement, H.D.L. Gordon had a two-thirds interest in the profit, and Dilworth one third. The business continued to expand, with Mr. Dilworth obtaining an increasing share of new work; a new agreement in April 1911 shared profits equally.

A clear indication of the growth and prosperity of the new firm can be found in its financial statements. For the year ending March 31, 1907, Robert Dilworth enjoyed a salary of $1,500 and a share of profits totalling about $1,000; Mr. Gordon's income was slightly larger. For the last ten months up to January 31, 1913 – the partnership's final period of operation – the statement reads as follows:

Net fees		$36,314.02
Expenses	$12,640.27	
Bad debts	451.60	
Commissions	340.46	
Depreciation, office furniture	199.29	
Bonus to Shiell and Taylor	1,062.84	14,694.46
		$21,619.56
To H.D.L. Gordon	$10,809.78	
R.J. Dilworth	10,809.78	
	$21,619.56	

This was indeed a creditable showing for ten months, given the short tenure of the partnership (not quite six years) and taking into consideration the value of the dollar at that time. The other names in the statement refer to Robert Shiell and W.D. Taylor, two young Scottish accountants who joined the firm in 1908 and would play an important role in a later partnership.

The firm Gordon & Dilworth was dissolved on January 31, 1913. The two partners then joined forces with the Clarksons – a key step in the present firm's evolution and the first pairing of the two surnames that today are inextricably linked.

II

Early in 1913, Geoffrey T. Clarkson, faced with the imminent retirement of W.H. Cross, met with H.D.L. Gordon and proposed that he take over management of the accounting practice at Clarkson & Cross. H.D.L. Gordon turned down this offer but said that he would be glad to rejoin the Clarkson firm as a full partner, provided that Robert Dilworth was offered the same terms. This proposal appealed to Geoffrey Clarkson, and a new partnership arrangement was soon worked out. The new firm was to be known as Clarkson, Gordon & Dilworth and would carry on the accounting practices of both firms. The four partners were

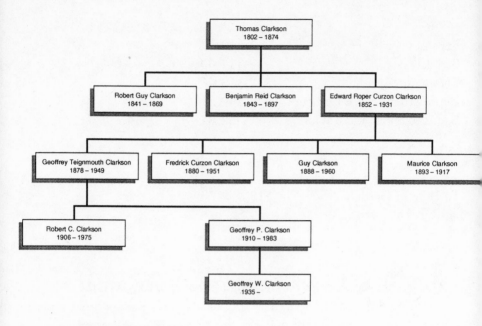

The Clarkson family

Geoffrey Clarkson, his father, E.R.C. Clarkson (then aged sixty), H.D.L. Gordon and Robert Dilworth. As part of the agreement, Gordon & Dilworth transferred all of its trustee and bankruptcy work to the Clarksons, who began to operate this portion of the business under the name E.R.C. Clarkson & Sons. (The practice of establishing a separate firm to handle the insolvency work was carried on in later years with the formation of The Clarkson Company, renamed Clarkson Gordon Inc. in 1985.) Joining E.R.C. Clarkson as partners in the insolvency firm were his sons Frederick, Guy and Geoffrey.

Geoffrey Teignmouth Clarkson, the eldest of the three brothers, was born in Toronto on October 21, 1878. He was educated at the Model School and Jarvis Collegiate, completing his formal education at the age of fifteen. Because he was too young to be accepted at university, he decided to go to work instead and joined his father's firm in 1893.

In business, Geoffrey Clarkson's two main specialties became bankruptcy work and the auditing of chartered banks. Through

24

G.T. Clarkson

the years, he gained a formidable reputation as a trustee, liquidator and assignee in many important insolvency cases. Much of the method of bankruptcy practice, and indeed much of the legislation created to deal with insolvencies, stem from principles that he established. He was also an acknowledged expert on banking and at one time was the auditor of five different banks in Toronto – the Imperial, Toronto, Dominion, Standard and Metropolitan. A 1923 amendment to the federal Bank Act, however, precluded a bank auditor from accepting special assignments from the institutions that he audited, and it became necessary for Mr. Clarkson to resign his bank audits. He appeared on numerous occasions before the Senate Banking and Finance Committees dealing with periodic revisions to the Bank Act, and was

25

considered an especially useful witness. The firm continues today as a major player in the auditing of and provision of advice to Canadian financial institutions. It counts many of the largest institutions as ongoing clients.

A rather shy and retiring man in private life, Geoffrey Clarkson enjoyed a great love of the outdoors. As a boy, he had been granted a licence by the Province of Ontario to collect birds' eggs, moths, fish life and other specimens on Toronto Island "for scientific purposes". (His father had a cottage on what is now Centre Island and in fact owned most of the island.) He remained an ardent naturalist throughout his life and became well known for his superb gardens in Wychwood Park, with their collections of rare species from all over the world.

In the early days, Geoffrey Clarkson and his brothers were highly respected aquatic competitors. His main sport was canoeing and, when in training, he used to paddle around Toronto Island. In later years, he loved to fish and shoot at his cottage in Muskoka. He also maintained a lifelong interest in education. He guided Havergal College as Vice-Chairman of its Board for many years, particularly during the difficult early 1930s; in addition, he was Vice-Chairman of Wycliffe College and a governor of Upper Canada College.

Geoffrey T. Clarkson died in 1949, in his seventy-first year. The elder of his two sons, Robert C. Clarkson, was with The Clarkson Company during the 1930s; the younger, Geoffrey P. Clarkson, became a distinguished partner of the firm. One grandson and one great-grandson have also carried on the family tradition: Geoffrey W. Clarkson (grandson of Geoffrey T. Clarkson) and Ronald J. Bogart (grandson of Geoffrey T. Clarkson's eldest daughter).

III

The outbreak of war in 1914 had a considerable impact on the newly founded firm Clarkson, Gordon & Dilworth and, in particular, on the career of H.D.L. Gordon. Mr. Gordon's early interest in riding, coupled with his training at the Royal Military

H.D.L. Gordon, "The Colonel"

College, had led to a longstanding involvement with the Toronto Mounted Rifles, which later became the Toronto Light Horse and finally the Mississauga Horse. At the time war was declared, he held the rank of Colonel and, as commander of the regiment, immediately went on active service.

In the fall of 1914, the 4th Canadian Mounted Rifle Regiment was formed, with units drawn from a number of other regiments. Colonel Gordon reverted to the rank of Major to take charge of "B" squadron and go overseas. He assumed command of the 4th Canadian Mounted Rifles in 1916 and fought with distinction in many battles, including Vimy Ridge. Among the honours he received were the Distinguished Service Order and the Volunteer Officer's Decoration. He was wounded in 1918 and returned to Canada before the end of the war.

Thereafter known as "the Colonel" to everyone in the firm, he remained an avid rider well into his seventies. He kept his own horses for much of that time and is remembered for being particularly fond of his horse "Buddy," which he owned for eighteen years. He was always a very active man. A good footballer at school, he played for Osgoode Hall after graduating from R.M.C. (although how this was arranged is not entirely certain). As a boy, he had been keenly interested in sailing, and he kept up this sport after graduation until the time of his marriage; at one point he was co-owner of a boat on Toronto bay that won several annual races at the Royal Canadian Yacht Club. He also enjoyed both trout and salmon fishing, which he took up seriously in his sixties.

Colonel Gordon was involved throughout his career in community affairs. For many years, he was active in the Order of St. John of Jerusalem, and for his good work he was made a Knight of the Order in 1934. He was also keenly interested in St. James's Cathedral in Toronto and played a key role in its administration, particularly with regard to investments and financial matters. Like his partners Geoffrey Clarkson and Robert Dilworth, he was always deeply involved in the development of the accounting profession; he served on the Council of the Ontario Institute and was its President in 1933–4.

It is safe to say, however, that Colonel Gordon's greatest interest, next to his family, was the practice itself. He was, for many years, a Senior Executive Partner, and he retained a direct involvement in management into his eighties. In business, he was hard-working and a strong motivator, providing the driving force behind the firm's growth following the First World War. He also set high standards of professional conduct, adhering to a strict code of right and wrong in business practice.

When Colonel Gordon went overseas with his regiment in 1914, R.J. Dilworth, then aged forty-five, was left to direct the new firm's accounting practice single-handedly. In spite of his heavy work load, he found time to join a reserve unit of the Queen's Own Rifles and qualified as a Lieutenant. Like his partners, he was keenly interested in the development of the profession, serving two terms as President of the Ontario Institute. He was also an incorporator, as well as one of the first directors, of the Canadian Society of Cost Accountants, which held its inaugural meeting at 15 Wellington Street West in 1920. (It is now the Society of Management Accountants of Canada.) The eldest of his four children, Ralph Dilworth, joined him in the firm and later became a partner. Robert Dilworth died on March 18, 1943.

IV

The formation of Clarkson, Gordon & Dilworth in 1913 was undoubtedly the single most important event in the history of the firm after its founding by Thomas Clarkson some five decades earlier. The three principal partners, Geoffrey T. Clarkson, Colonel Gordon and R.J. Dilworth, were well known and respected in the business community. Each had highly developed professional skills, a wealth of experience and a wide circle of friends and acquaintances. Even given this potent combination of attributes, however, they could have had no idea just how successful their newly launched venture was to be.

CHAPTER FOUR

Through War and Peace: 1913-1945

THE THIRTY OR SO YEARS following the formation of Clarkson, Gordon & Dilworth and E.R.C. Clarkson & Sons in 1913 saw tremendous growth for both firms, as well as for the profession generally. It was also a turbulent period in Canadian history, spanning the Great War of 1914–18, the recession of the 1920s, the devastating depression of the next decade and the Second World War, 1939–45. The first fiscal year of the new operation, however, was a great success and promised even more for the future: fee revenue from the accounting practice was substantially increased over the combined previous year's totals for the two merged firms.

Colonel Gordon went overseas in late 1914 and was soon followed by Guy Clarkson and several other colleagues, all of whom remained overseas for the duration of the war. The work load for those left behind was correspondingly heavy, with R.J. Dilworth carrying most of the burden as senior partner on the accounting side, and his counterpart Geoffrey T. Clarkson handling the trustee work and various special assignments.

The affiliated firm of E.R.C. Clarkson & Sons originally had very few permanent employees; temporary staff members were hired on a daily basis as the volume of trustee and bankruptcy work demanded. E.R.C. Clarkson remained a partner until his death in 1931, but as he became less active in later years, his place at the head of the firm was taken by his son Geoffrey. The other two sons, Fred and Guy, worked with their older brother throughout the period between the wars. Maurice Clarkson, a younger brother born in 1893, worked for the firm briefly before the First World War. He was killed in action at Vimy Ridge.

II

On April 1, 1913, the newly merged firm of Clarkson, Gordon & Dilworth acquired offices on the top floor of the Merchants Bank Building in Toronto. This architectural landmark, located at 15 Wellington Street West, was to remain the firm's headquarters for the next fifty-six years.

By 1920, the accounting firm's business had expanded substantially and more space was required. At the same time, the management of the Merchants Bank wished to move to King Street and was interested in selling the building. Colonel Gordon and Robert Dilworth, apparently after some spirited bargaining, negotiated the bank's asking price down from $137,500 to $112,500, of which $40,029 was attributed to the land. The purchase agreement stipulated that the new owners "will not use or permit the said premises to be used for banking purposes", while the property description provided for the free and uninterrupted use of an adjacent laneway for "carts, vehicles, carriages, horses or cattle as by them should be convenient at all times and seasons".

Accounting work during the years 1914–18 was affected materially – just as it would be during the Second World War – by the passage of special tax legislation. The Special War Revenue Act of 1915, the Business Profits War Tax Act of 1916 and the Income War Tax Act of 1917 all created new problems for the taxpayers of Canada and their advisers. On his return from overseas in 1918, Colonel Gordon was quick to recognize the continuing potential in special tax work; he ensured that the firm was equipped to handle it by appointing several new partners and seeking out opportunities for expansion.

In 1922, Robert Shiell, who had joined the firm fourteen years earlier and had since become a partner (and the brother-in-law of Colonel Gordon), moved to Montreal to open an office in the name of Clarkson, Gordon & Dilworth. Unfortunately, he died suddenly in 1927, and it became necessary to make new arrangements for

The Board Room and Mr. Fred Clarkson

the Montreal practice. An approach was made to George C. McDonald and his partner George Currie, who had been practising together, as McDonald, Currie & Co., in Montreal since 1910 (except for a brief period of service overseas during the war). These two first cousins – both good friends of Colonel Gordon and his partners – had built up a successful practice and were well known and respected in the community. As of April 1, 1928, an arrangement was worked out under which the combined practice in Quebec and the Maritimes would be carried out by the firm of Clarkson, McDonald, Currie & Co., while Ontario and the west continued to be served by Clarkson, Gordon & Dilworth (which soon changed its name to Clarkson, Gordon, Dilworth, Guilfoyle & Nash). During their period together, the two firms retained a good degree of autonomy, but it was undoubtedly hoped that a single, large firm would emerge. This, however, was not to be, and in 1935 the partnership was dissolved, with each of the old firms reopening its own office in Montreal. (McDonald, Currie & Co. continues today as Coopers & Lybrand.)

The surnames of Harvey Guilfoyle and Albert Nash were added

33

to the firm's Ontario name in 1928. Harvey Edward Guilfoyle, born in 1887 in Lucan, Ontario, had joined the firm of Gordon & Dilworth in 1912. He was keenly interested in the profession and, in addition to heading both the Ontario Institute and the Dominion Association, was also President of the Society of Industrial & Cost Accountants of Canada. During the First World War, he served overseas as an officer in the 9th Mississauga Horse; he returned to the firm in June 1918 and became a partner three years later. In 1935, at the age of forty-eight, Harvey Guilfoyle died suddenly while on assignment for the firm in New Brunswick. (The firm name was subsequently changed to Clarkson, Gordon, Dilworth & Nash.) His son, Harold Guilfoyle, later became a partner in the associated consulting firm, Woods, Gordon & Co.

Albert Edward Nash, born in England in 1884, was articled to a firm of chartered accountants before coming to Canada in 1907. He settled in Edmonton and shortly afterward began to practise as an accountant, forming his own firm, Nash & Nash. In the First World War he enlisted as a private and was commissioned with the 19th Alberta Dragoons; he was awarded the Military Cross overseas and returned home as a Major. Having decided to remain in eastern Canada after the war, he joined the firm in 1921 and became a partner four years later. He resumed his military career during the Second World War and, at the time of his death in 1944, held the rank of Major-General.

III

During the period from 1913 to 1938, the firm opened four new offices, two of which were later closed. Representation in Montreal, as we have seen, dates from 1922. In 1929, offices were established in Windsor and Ottawa. The former was intended primarily to provide local service to one major client and was closed five years later. The Ottawa office, set up to facilitate business in the federal capital, continued until 1937. These offices were subsequently re-opened after the Second World War. The Hamilton office, opened in 1938, remains a key Ontario office.

The collapse of the stock market in 1929 precipitated the greatest depression in modern times. Thousands of men and women were thrown out of their jobs, families became destitute and factories lay idle. In an effort to retain personnel, the firm extended the annual vacation period for staff members from two to three weeks (without pay), which kept an additional two people employed. Times were hard, however, even for those who managed to find employment. Many of the retired partners still recall the "Dirty Thirties" and the modest salaries they earned — but most staff members were thankful just to be working. When Jack Biddell (later President of The Clarkson Company Limited) began with the firm, he carried on his daily paper route because he needed the extra money to support himself.

Despite the depression, the 1930s saw a significant increase in business. The firm was engaged in regular audit work for various departments and commissions of the Ontario government; at the same time, Geoffrey T. Clarkson, in particular, was doing a great deal of work for the chartered banks. Professional staff at the two firms grew from about 15 people in 1913 to roughly 115 by 1938. In the same period, the total number of chartered accountants in Canada rose from 375 to 2,220 — an increase clearly out of proportion to the general growth in population during those years (though the rate of increase in the profession slowed significantly during the 1930s, when money and jobs were scarce, just as it did later, during the disruptive years of the Second World War).

By 1938, only 63 per cent of Canadian chartered accountants were engaged in public practice (a proportion that has remained fairly constant throughout the century); that the remaining 37 per cent were employed in other pursuits is a clear indication of the rising demand for highly trained financial and accounting personnel in commerce and industry. This demand can be attributed to the same factors that underlay the growth of the firm in this twenty-five year period: the increasing complexity of modern business finance, the proliferation of government rules and regulations, the need for greater disclosure of accurate information and the intricacy of accounting problems created by various new forms of taxation.

The Second World War disrupted the lives and livelihoods of all Canadians, and those in accounting firms were no exception. At that time, a typical firm's staff was composed primarily of intelligent, healthy young men between the ages of eighteen and thirty; naturally, the armed forces and government services relied heavily on people of this sort for the war effort.

During the course of the war, 116 men and women left Clarkson, Gordon, Dilworth & Nash to serve in the armed forces – a significant number, considering that in 1939 the professional staff of the firm's three offices in Toronto, Montreal and Hamilton totalled 139. Many did not return, among them Colonel Gordon's son Hugh, an Air Force officer, and Hugh Glassco, brother of senior partner Grant Glassco. Also missed by his co-workers was Billy Wallace, the firm's young office boy, who was killed in action as a Pilot Officer.

In addition to service with the armed forces, many members of the firm contributed to important war work on the home front. Walter Gordon, eldest son of the Colonel and a partner in the firm, went to Ottawa to assist in setting up the Foreign Exchange Control Board and later became a Special Assistant to the Deputy Minister of Finance. Grant Glassco received a government appointment as Controller, and later Financial Administrator, of Clyde Aircraft Limited, a Collingwood firm that found itself in financial difficulties at a time when it was making urgently needed components for the Valentine Tank. Mr. Glassco was subsequently appointed Controller of De Havilland Aircraft Company, which was taken over by the federal government.

Geoffrey P. Clarkson (younger son of Geoffrey T. Clarkson and grandson of E.R.C. Clarkson) went to New York to serve in the financial section of the British Purchasing Commission. Later, he and Walter Gordon returned to work full-time with J.D. Woods Company, which had been loaned to the Division for Simplification of Industry, part of the federal government's War Time Prices and Trade Board. (J.D. Woods Company would later evolve into the consulting firm Woods, Gordon & Co.)

The problems of the firm, serious enough because of staff turnover, were compounded by the tremendous increase in special work brought on by wartime conditions. Of particular importance was the preparation of numerous briefs for submission to the Board of Referees under the Excess Profits Tax Act and, when necessary, appearances before the Board. Special assignments also arose out of orders regarding Salary and Wage Control, Price Control and similar wartime measures, as well as costing work under war contracts. The heavy work-load accelerated the move toward greater reliance on test audits and internal control. It also led to the first recruitment of women as audit clerks.

The introduction of about fifty female staff members – known as Lady Audit Clerks, or L.A.C.s – into a hitherto all-male environment proved a great success. The young women quickly showed themselves to be as intelligent and hard-working as their male counterparts. To assist them in learning the fundamentals of auditing, the firm prepared a series of intensive lecture courses followed by written tests. These lectures were subsequently published in the *Chartered Accountant* magazine and made available in booklet form to other practitioners. From such lecture courses, Bert Dell and Jack Wilson, two senior partners in the firm, produced one of the first Canadian auditing textbooks, *Principles of Auditing* (but known universally as "Dell and Wilson"). In its day, this textbook was used by most accounting students in the country.

Unfortunately, the time was not yet right for the acceptance and encouragement of women in the profession. A few of the firm's female staff members started the C.A. course of instruction, but only three carried on to graduate as chartered accountants – all enjoying great success. One of these was Gertrude Mulcahy, a great-great-granddaughter of the firm's founder, Thomas Clarkson, through his first child, Betsy, born in England in 1823 before he came to Canada. Gertrude Mulcahy is still active in the field and is currently a member of Council in the Institute of Chartered Accountants of Ontario.

Those men and women who were on active service received "The Clarkson Dispatch," a mimeographed newsletter designed to keep the firm in touch with its absent staff members and to provide some welcome news from home. The first issue came out in November 1941 as "The Clarkson War Cry" but was promptly renamed out of concern that it might be mistaken for a contemporary publication with a similar name; eight further issues appeared, as news required, until April 1945. The firm, meanwhile, not only endeavoured to keep in touch with its members in the services but also purchased War Savings Certificates for them each month they were away.

During these years, the firm grew moderately in size, despite the difficulty of recruiting qualified personnel. And, while no additional offices were opened until after the war, an important new dimension was added with the formation of an international partnership: Arthur Young, Clarkson, Gordon & Co. A friendly and rewarding relationship had existed for some time with the American firm Arthur Young & Company; in 1944, the new joint firm was established to conduct business in Canada for Arthur Young & Company and in the United States for Clarkson, Gordon & Co.

CHAPTER FIVE

A Truly National Firm

As CANADIAN TROOPS began returning from overseas in 1945, the moderate wartime growth of Clarkson, Gordon, Dilworth & Nash gave way to an era of rapid expansion. Reflective of this new momentum was the decision, in early 1946, to change the name of the firm to Clarkson, Gordon & Co. – the form it was to take for the next thirty-four years. At the same time, the trustee and bankruptcy business, E.R.C. Clarkson & Sons, became the Clarkson Company partnership.

The renewed growth of the firm during the post-war period, though in percentage terms not as dramatic as the years from 1913 to 1938, brought strength and diversity through the opening of offices across the country and the addition of partners and staff as a result of many mergers. The chief initiators of this vigorous program of expansion were two senior partners, whose experience, vision and stature in the business community were of vital importance to the evolution of the firm: Grant Glassco and Walter Gordon.

John Grant Glassco was born in Los Angeles on January 20, 1905, and spent his formative years in Winnipeg. A graduate of McGill University, he continued his education at the Sorbonne in Paris on a Province of Quebec scholarship. On returning to Canada, he decided to study for his C.A. designation, and in 1926 he joined McDonald, Currie & Co. (now Coopers & Lybrand) in Montreal; the following year he was moved to its Quebec City office. During these years, the Montreal firm was involved in the partnership Clarkson, McDonald, Currie & Co., and, as a consequence, Grant Glassco was sent to Toronto under an exchange arrangement that took Walter Gordon to Montreal. When the joint venture was dissolved in 1935, Mr. Glassco remained in Toronto and became a partner of Clarkson, Gordon, Dilworth & Nash.

While most widely known as a tax specialist, Grant Glassco was a well-rounded accountant whose professional expertise earned him an international reputation. He devoted a great deal of time and energy to the development of the profession in Canada, serving as President of the Institute of Chartered Accountants of Ontario in 1948–9 and heading the Canadian Institute of Chartered Accountants (CICA) in 1954–5. In 1957, Grant Glassco left the firm to become President of Brazilian Traction, Light and Power Company, Ltd. (now Brascan Limited), a position he held until his retirement. He died in 1968.

Walter Lockhart Gordon, the Colonel's eldest son, was born in 1906 and educated at Upper Canada College and the Royal Military College. An excellent athlete in both track and football, he spent the first year after graduation playing as a halfback with the Toronto Argonaut football team. He joined the family firm in 1927 and became a partner in 1935. From the outset, he took an active interest in the management of the firm, eventually succeeding his father as Senior Partner. He was instrumental in forging the first links with J.D. Woods & Co. in 1939 and directed the consulting firm from 1942 until his retirement in 1963.

In the years following the Second World War, Walter Gordon – more than any other partner – was responsible for setting the policies of both firms and providing the initiative that fuelled their expansion. "Walter was the real brain behind the organization," one partner later recalled. "He had the breadth of vision to select the right people and make sure that those people did what they should be doing to expand the firm." A great many special assignments and investigations of various kinds were either conducted or supervised by him. He also headed a number of royal commissions and special committees of the federal and Ontario governments. Foremost among these was the Royal Commission

40

J. Grant Glassco

on Canada's Economic Prospects (1955–7), which resulted in the famous "Gordon Report."

Walter Gordon was an ardent nationalist and throughout his career became increasingly determined that control of Canadian companies remain in Canadian hands. He saw the need for a Canadian holding company, one close associate explained, to act "as an alternative purchaser of Canadian companies whose owners were forced by circumstances to sell." Attempts to set up such a company before the war were unsuccessful, but soon after the war, Mr. Gordon spearheaded the creation of Canadian Corporate Management Company Limited, which later became Canadian Corporate Management. Over the years, Canadian Corporate

Management proved a major success, and, until it was sold in 1986 (to Canadians, of course), Mr. Gordon took pride in the fact that his company was at least partially reversing the trend toward foreign takeovers of Canadian businesses.

In 1946, Walter Gordon was made a Commander of the Order of the British Empire (C.B.E.) in recognition of his distinguished wartime service with the federal government. Always interested in cultural and community affairs, he took on a variety of public posts, including the Presidency of the Toronto Board of Trade (1947), a governorship of the University of Toronto and the Chair of the National Executive Committee of the Canadian Institute of International Affairs. In the federal election of 1962, he won the riding of Toronto-Davenport for the Liberal Party. The next year, he was re-elected and resigned from both the accounting and consulting firms to become Minister of Finance in the government of Prime Minister Lester Pearson.

Following his retirement from politics in the late 1960s, Mr. Gordon helped establish the influential Committee for an Independent Canada, which embodied his strong views on the need for a national policy of economic independence; he later added his voice to the campaigns for arms control and nuclear disarmament.

Walter Gordon's political career revealed only one side of his character to the people of Canada. A man of integrity and enormous energy, he was able to juggle several demanding careers simultaneously. He led by example and was a superb judge of character. Perhaps his greatest contribution to the firm, therefore, should be measured not in statistics or on a balance sheet but rather in the quality of those people he chose to succeed him.

II

The surge of oil from the frozen ground near the town of Leduc, Alberta, in February 1947, ushered in a new era in the history of western Canada. The presence of oil fields in Alberta had been known since the end of the First World War, but exploitation of this enormous energy resource had to wait until 1945. The post-war economic boom in North America needed energy to feed

Walter L. Gordon

its industries and to fuel its transportation. The eyes of Canadian business turned to the west.

Within a generation, the emergence of the oil industry revolutionized the economy of Alberta and the whole of western Canada. The exploration, production and transmission of oil sparked the rapid growth of Calgary and Edmonton as administrative and financial headquarters that rivalled the cities of eastern Canada. As the growth of the resource sector attracted other industries and people to the region, the stunning rise in the world price of oil made the Alberta "oil patch" the envy of the world.

For Clarkson, Gordon, the expansion of the western economy offered tremendous opportunities. As existing clients moved into dynamic areas of new growth, the firm needed a western presence to serve them. Moreover, the rise of new businesses in western Canada produced a whole new range of potential clients. The opportunity was not squandered: within twenty-five years Clarkson, Gordon had spread across the country to become a truly national firm.

Since the dissolution of Clarkson, Cross & Helliwell in 1910, the firm had been represented in Vancouver but had not maintained an office of its own. In 1945, just as the war was drawing to a close, Grant Ross of the Toronto office moved to Vancouver to re-establish the practice on the west coast. Mr. Ross had joined the firm in 1933 and became a partner in 1945. Though still one of the younger members of the firm, he assumed full responsibility for building up the western practice. Mr. Ross remained in Vancouver until 1953, when he returned to Toronto. He retired in 1977.

The development of a strong client base is never an easy task, especially when a new office is opened in a particularly competitive market. In Vancouver, the large resource industries and other important companies already had auditors, and the new Clarkson, Gordon office could not rely on reputation alone to attract new clients; a whole new clientele had to be developed slowly from the ground up. "You could not just walk into this city, or any other large city," one Vancouver partner explained, "and suddenly create a presence for yourself, no matter what your name was. There were too many large local firms here who had already established a presence and were auditing all the large corporations."

In addition to attracting new clients to the firm, strategic mergers with strong local firms helped to augment the client base. In 1948, a merger was arranged in Vancouver with the local practice of Harold Campbell, who continued for a time as a consultant with the firm. Eleven years later, in 1959, the Vancouver partnership of Carter, Reid & Walden merged with the firm. Mr. Carter (a former Chief Assessor with the Department of National Revenue in Vancouver) carried on as a consultant after the merger; his colleagues Alexander Reid and Frank Walden became partners of Clarkson, Gordon.

Under the leadership of such Office Managing Partners as

George Donaldson, Frank Walden, Bonar Lund, Henry Pankratz and Ken Cross, the Vancouver practice has made steady progress. Henry Pankratz was the first Vancouver partner appointed to the Executive Committee of the firm. The office has shown strong growth in the last few years and has undertaken significant government work, including a 1976 report on the financial condition of British Columbia after the Social Credit Party replaced the New Democratic Party as the provincial government.

A logical area for expansion in British Columbia was to Victoria, the provincial capital. In 1967, a merger was arranged with the local firm Holt & Campion, which had already been acting as agents for Clarkson, Gordon for several years. Today the practice is led by Vern Fitzgerald, the Office Managing Partner. Victoria remains a small office, looking after a number of national clients (such as Eaton's) and many local businesses and professional people on Vancouver Island. Tax work and financial advice are the bread and butter of the practice; in addition, some work for the provincial government has been undertaken.

The situation in Winnipeg after the war was similar to that of Vancouver: the firm had local representation but had not maintained an office in its own name since the dissolution of Clarkson, Cross & Menzies in 1913. Through a 1948 merger with the practice of Black, Hanson & Co., a Winnipeg office was added to the growing network. Over the years, Winnipeg has been a very strong contributor to the firm, in terms of both financial results and strong partners for other practice units. The office has had strong leadership from Bill Shields, Al Moore and Ralph Palmer. Al Moore retired in 1988, after thirty-one years in Winnipeg, having moved west from Hamilton in 1957. He has been called the "ultimate business developer", and it is said that he knows virtually everyone in town.

The following year, 1949, brought another key merger, this time with the Calgary firm Richardson & Graves. Eric Richardson had established his practice in 1917 and since 1932 had been in partnership with Mervyn Graves. From April 1, 1949, the two men conducted business as the Calgary office of Clarkson, Gordon & Co., with Mr. Richardson as a consultant and Mr. Graves as a

Mervyn Graves

partner in the firm. In 1956, the Calgary firm Macintosh & Ross was dissolved and William Macintosh joined Clarkson, Gordon & Co.; Mr. Macintosh brought many important new clients to the firm, including Pacific Petroleum, Westcoast Transmission, the Alberta Wheat Pool and Alberta Distillers. In 1960, the Calgary office merged once more, this time with the respected firm of Harvey, Morrison & Company, established in 1924.

Much of the significant growth in the Calgary practice came under the leadership of Don McGregor and John Rooney. Mr. McGregor worked in the Calgary office from 1949 until his retirement in 1979 and served as President of the Alberta Institute of Chartered Accountants (1961–2). Mr. Rooney worked in the Calgary office from 1959 until his untimely death in January

46

Don McGregor

1983. In addition to his many years as Office Managing Partner, Mr. Rooney served as President of the Alberta Institute of Chartered Accountants (1968–9), and in later years was an Executive Partner of Clarkson, Gordon. Glen Cronkwright, who moved from Toronto to Calgary in 1982, took over the reins as Office Managing Partner from Crawford Smith and continued as the Executive Partner in western Canada.

The evolution of the Calgary office has paralleled the dynamic growth of the economy of Alberta. In 1964, there were 7 partners and a total staff of 51; by the middle of 1988, these numbers had risen to 28 partners and over 220 total staff. Some of the office's most important clients – including NOVA, Transalta Utilities, Mobil Oil, BP Canada and Gulf Canada – rank among the largest

John Rooney

corporations in Canada. Today, under the direction of Dave
Finlay, the Office Managing Partner, Calgary is the third largest
office (behind Toronto and Montreal). The audit practice, led by
Glen Braum, is the largest practice area. The office has a large
consulting practice, led by Bill Best, a tax group of more than
twenty professionals, led by John Lowden, and a substantial
insolvency practice under the leadership of Ron Isaac.

An Edmonton office was added in 1956. The local firm of
Kinnaird, Aylen & Co. traced its beginnings to 1910, when
George Johnstone Kinnaird, an emigrant from Dundee, Scotland,
opened a public practice specializing in municipal accounting. His
son, G.D.K. Kinnaird, took over after the First World War and
played a leading role in the firm until the merger of 1956 – at

which point he became a partner of Clarkson, Gordon & Co. Ken Kinnaird was the first white man born in Fort Athabasca (now Athabasca). Mr. Kinnaird tells this story in a letter to Edmonton partner Jack McMahon:

Fort Edmonton was the distributor of all supplies to the Northern Posts, once a year by the water route. All supplies were freighted overland to Fort Athabasca where scows (flat-bottomed boats) were constructed on the river bank. In the spring they were loaded and immediately after the ice moved out, the scows were launched to take advantage of the high water in the wake of the ice, the only time the scows could navigate the many rapids. In the Spring of 1891, my father was sent to Fort Athabasca to supervise the loading and launching of the scows. As there was no Doctor in Edmonton or Athabasca, my mother accompanied him. I was born in Fort Athabasca on May 25, 1891, the first white child to be born there. An Indian woman delivered me and my diet was augmented with hardtack soaked in water.

To assist him with the Edmonton practice, Bruce Mitchell moved from Hamilton in 1957 and continued to lead the practice in Edmonton until his death in 1976. In that year, Bob Lord moved to Edmonton, where he spent the next ten years as Office Managing Partner. In 1986, Mr. Lord returned to Toronto to become an Executive Partner and National Director of Accounting. Since then, the Edmonton practice has been directed by Les Tutty, as Office Managing Partner.

A Saskatchewan office was opened in 1952 through a merger with Read, Smith & Forbes of Regina. (The original practice had been established in 1913 by Walter Read, an English emigrant.) Other mergers followed. In 1968, the Regina office merged with Wicijowski, Wenaus & Co., which doubled the size of the practice. Gordon Wicijowski became the Office Managing Partner and has led the practice very successfully since that time. Another merger took place in 1975 with the firm Basin & Barsky. The Regina office is now the largest in that city, with major clients such as Saskatchewan Power Corporation, Crown Management

Board, Saskatchewan Oil and Gas Corporation, Credit Union Central and Harvard Developments Limited.

The Regina partners were instrumental in the opening of a Saskatoon office in 1979. The new office took over all of the firm's clients from northern Saskatchewan, an area seen as ripe for expansion. Both Saskatchewan offices have since evolved into full-service practices with national and multinational clients.

An office in Thunder Bay, Ontario, was also established during these early years. When the Winnipeg office opened in 1948, Harold S. Hanson, of Black, Hanson & Co., became a partner in Clarkson, Gordon & Co. His partner, Francis Henry Black, declined the offer and continued to practice in the Fort William-Port Arthur (now Thunder Bay) area. Mr. Black retired in 1965, and two years later, the remaining partners of F.H. Black & Co. merged with Clarkson, Gordon & Co. Mr. Black, who had been made an Officer of the Order of the British Empire (O.B.E.) in 1946, made a distinguished contribution to the firm as a consulting partner until his death in 1970. Ken Bruley, who entered the firm through the merger, moved to Toronto and then to St. John's for five years, returning to Thunder Bay as Office Managing Partner.

III

In the late 1940s, southwestern Ontario was perceived increasingly as an area of tremendous potential growth. To take advantage of that potential, the firm opened an office in London in August 1948. Until then, the firm's London clients had been served by the Toronto office. They included London Life Insurance Co., John Labatt Ltd. and Canada and Dominion Sugar Co.

The new London office was staffed by personnel from Toronto under the supervision of Ken Lemon. Mr. Lemon joined the firm in 1936 (at a starting salary, he recalled later with some amusement, of forty dollars a month) and moved to London in 1948 to become Managing Partner – a post he held for more than twenty-five years. Under the leadership of Ken Lemon and John Robinson (who later followed Mr. Lemon as an Executive Partner),

Ken Lemon

the London office experienced remarkable growth and went on to become by far the largest firm in that city. Today, the London office consists of nineteen partners, bringing the total number of staff close to 200. The present group of senior partners includes Bruce Beckett, Doug McDonald and Bill Wood, who are all products of Ken Lemon's tenure in the firm.

Alliances with two respected firms in southwestern Ontario helped further to extend the Clarkson, Gordon presence in 1962. The first of these was Davis, Dunn and Broughton (founded in the early 1930s), which had offices in Kitchener and London. The second Kitchener-based firm to merge that year was Scully & Scully, which boasted a long history dating back to about 1850. (George Richardson, a senior partner of Clarkson, Gordon, had trained as a student with this firm.) The two mergers brought Bruce Davis, Kenneth Dunn, John Broughton and Donald Scully into the partnership. Under the leadership of Ron Gage, Howie Jasper and John Cowperthwaite, the Kitchener office has evolved into a well-rounded practice, with a broad range of large and small clients.

The Hamilton office, established before the war, underwent a period of rapid expansion after 1945, thanks largely to the sustained efforts of four managing partners over fifty years: Ted Ambrose, Harold Dixon, Bill Wilson and Barry Nicol. Ted Ambrose became the first Hamilton partner in the early 1940s and, apart from taking an executive position with Dofasco from 1947 to 1950, was Managing Partner until his death in 1967. He was one of the founders of the Hamilton Foundation and Chairman of the Board of Governors of McMaster University. Harold Dixon joined the Toronto office in 1932 and became a partner in 1947, at which time he transferred to the Hamilton office. By the time of Mr. Dixon's retirement in 1975, Clarkson, Gordon's practice was the largest in the Hamilton area. This position has been maintained under the direction of Barry Nicol; the office has a number of major clients, including Dofasco Inc., the New Harding Group Inc. and Fleet Aerospace Corporation.

Expansion during these years was not restricted to Canada. In 1959, a special partnership was formed in Brazil, bringing together Arthur Young & Co. (with which the firm had been associated for some time) and Henry Martin & Co. of Uruguay. With offices in Rio de Janeiro and São Paulo, the Brazilian partnership of Arthur Young, Clarkson, Gordon & Co. set out to build upon the base established by the Canadian firm as auditors of Brazilian Traction, Light and Power and its affiliated companies. (This relationship dated back to the turn of the century, when Clarkson & Cross was auditing the Toronto-based São Paulo Tramway, Light and Power Company.)

At the same time, overall relations between Clarkson, Gordon and Arthur Young (U.S.) were steadily strengthening. Indeed, according to David Wishart, a Clarkson, Gordon partner who became the first Executive Partner of Arthur Young International, "it was the satisfactory nature of this relationship (and a similar relationship with a firm in London, England – now Arthur Young

(U.K.) – dating back to 1923) that persuaded AY (U.S.) to seek out relationships with strong local firms in other countries to serve its clients, rather than opening offices in other countries. This remains the underlying philosophy of AYI to this day." In 1964, the various firms that had ties with AY (U.S.) formed Arthur Young & Company (International), known today as Arthur Young International. For many years, the Gordon brothers maintained fierce independence in the firm's international dealings, but in recent years Clarkson Gordon's working relationship with the world of AYI (particularly the American firm) has become much closer.

Trustee work also continued to grow in importance throughout the post-war period. In 1954, the Clarkson Company partnership was dissolved and its business transferred to a newly formed corporation, The Clarkson Company Limited.

In 1946, the two Clarkson firms and the associated consulting firm of J.D. Woods & Gordon Ltd. had a total staff, including administrative personnel, of 200 people working in four offices. By 1963, on the eve of the Clarkson, Gordon centennial, there were 900 staff members in twelve offices, and the number of partners had grown from twenty to ninety-two.

CHAPTER SIX

The Woods Gordon
Connection

B Y THE LATE 1930s, the accountancy prac-
tice was dealing with more and more clients whose business
problems were only indirectly connected with accounting and
financial matters. It became apparent that the firm would either
have to take on staff members with a wider range of skills or join
forces with an organization that possessed those skills already. The
solution came in the form of a small but innovative consulting
company that was to evolve, under the initial guidance of Walter
Gordon, into a vital complement to the Clarkson, Gordon team
and an unquestioned leader in management consulting.

The organization that became Woods, Gordon & Co. had its
rather modest beginnings in the time-study department of a
Toronto textile manufacturer, York Knitting Mills Limited. In
the late 1920s, Douglas Woods, then President of York Knitting
Mills, was approached by the American industrial engineering
firm Charles E. Bedaux Co. with a plan to improve his company's
performance by introducing a wage-incentive plan. The Bedaux
team worked for two years implementing the new system and
during that time trained a York Knitting executive, Ralph
Presgrave, to carry on after it left. Mr. Presgrave subsequently
made improvements on the plan, as well as on the time-study
method on which it was based. He also built up a staff of industrial
engineers to introduce the plan at other textile plants that the
manufacturer had acquired in Hamilton and Woodstock, Ontario.

The techniques developed under the direction of Ralph
Presgrave (whose success soon earned him an international

J. Douglas Woods

reputation) were seen to be at least as effective as anything promoted by engineering firms in the United States; the time seemed right, therefore, for a Canadian firm to enter the field. Accordingly, the firm J.D. Woods & Co. was founded in 1932 to take on work outside York Knitting Mills. The President of the new venture was Douglas Woods, with Ralph Presgrave as Vice-President.

These assignments remained in the textile industry at first, where the J.D. Woods staff had previous experience, and then broadened to a wider range of enterprises, particularly in metal working. The company also became more diversified in its activities. Initially, the main service offered consisted of training time-study specialists and helping them to set up incentive plans and labour controls; as time went on, the company's expertise

Ralph Presgrave

broadened to include systems and procedures, as well as sales and merchandising. Even with this expansion, however, staff members throughout the 1930s never totalled more than a dozen.

The association with Clarkson, Gordon dates from 1939, when the accounting firm's desire to provide more extensive services led to the formation of a joint venture, J.D. Woods Co. Limited. Walter Gordon, Grant Glassco and Clare A. Patterson were Clarkson, Gordon's representatives on the Board of Directors; Douglas Woods, his brother, William B. Woods, and Ralph Presgrave represented a group known as Woods Bros. & Associates. The disruption caused by the outbreak of war resulted in the two groups continuing to operate separately for the time being. The Woods group handled production and merchandising services from its offices at York Knitting Mills; a small number of consultants in the accounting firm directed systems and procedures services from 15 Wellington Street West.

In 1942, after enlistment in the armed forces had reduced the staff of The J.D. Woods Co. to a mere handful, Walter Gordon proposed that the entire firm be placed at the disposal of the federal government to aid in its program to conserve manpower and materials. He took over active direction of the firm and, from new offices in the Star Building (on King Street in Toronto), oversaw its expansion from a nucleus of five to a total of over thirty. During the next two years various studies were undertaken on behalf of the Canadian government. This work came to an end in late 1943, however, and the following year the new firm J.D. Woods and Gordon Ltd. was established. Only a few of those who had participated in the government work stayed with the firm, and, once again, the consulting firm – now sharing the accounting group's Wellington Street offices – faced the task of building up its professional staff.

During the post-war years, there was a growing demand for consulting services and a corresponding increase in J.D. Woods & Gordon staff members to about forty – a level maintained throughout the 1950s. The same period saw an inevitable broadening of the variety and scope of assignments undertaken, as well as in the range of clients served. The firm continued to provide extensive support in the production area, meeting growing demand for organization studies, marketing surveys, management control procedures, data processing systems and other innovative services. At the same time, the client base expanded beyond industry to include hospitals, professional associations, educational institutions and government at all levels.

As the firm changed, so too did its corporate structure. Douglas Woods ultimately became Chairman of the Board and Walter Gordon President, while the number of directors more than doubled from the original eight. On January 1, 1959, the firm ceased to be a limited company and became a partnership; Douglas Woods and Ralph Presgrave retired but continued to make a contribution as consulting partners.

By the early 1960s, a total staff of sixty people, including partners, senior consultants and consultants, shared offices with the accounting firm in Montreal, Toronto, London, Calgary and Vancouver. This close relationship with Clarkson, Gordon & Co., of vital importance since the two firms first came together, would grow steadily closer as professionals from both areas joined forces to solve the problems of clients across the country.

II

On October 1, 1960, Walter Gordon rose to speak at the annual meeting of the partners of the two firms. He began his remarks by noting that Clarkson, Gordon and Woods, Gordon were the two largest firms in Canada in their respective fields. "Of more importance," he continued, "I think our reputation in both fields for sound, imaginative and conscientious work is as high as or higher than that of any other firm." But the nature of business in Canada was changing, Mr. Gordon added, and this had affected the two firms: "Not only is our total business much larger than it used to be, it is also much more complex and varied. We have become, or are becoming, an association of specialists – accountants and auditors, experts in many fields of modern management techniques, trustees and receivers, tax experts, and consultants to businesses, to wealthy individuals and to all three levels of government upon occasion."

A new decade lay ahead, Mr. Gordon continued, and the firms must be prepared to meet the challenges and adapt to a changing environment. "Let all of us adopt a broad approach to all the work we do," he said. "We must not miss the forest for the trees. Let none of us hesitate to consult another partner before we offer advice or give opinions – this principle of getting a second opinion before we act is an imperative essential in the way in which our firms are organized and operated. And," he concluded, "let not one of us ever forget that our reputations individually, and those of our two firms, depend upon our maintaining the very highest standards of business morality in everything we do."

CHAPTER SEVEN

The Firm
at One Hundred

In 1964, THE FIRM CELEBRATED its one hundredth anniversary. In Toronto, a large formal dinner was held at the Royal York Hotel to honour the occasion, and it included speeches by several of the senior partners. All staff members were invited, of course, and invitations were extended also to all the alumni listed in the firm's directory. But the festivities were not confined to Toronto; indeed, there were celebrations all across the country. From Vancouver to Quebec City, each office marked the occasion in its own unique way.

The year 1964 was also significant, as it marked the end of one era and the beginning of another. Only a few months earlier, in July 1963, Colonel Gordon celebrated his ninetieth birthday. His partners presented him with ninety red roses and an illuminated salutation, a beautiful scroll in a leather cover, which read:

COLONEL H.D. LOCKHART GORDON

On this the twentieth of July in the year nineteen sixty-three
your seventy-four partners in Clarkson, Gordon & Co. join in
saluting their senior partner on his ninetieth birthday and in
extending the warmest of good wishes for the years ahead.

In April 1963, Walter Gordon retired from the firm and assumed his new post as federal Minister of Finance, after twenty-eight years as a partner. Under the leadership of Douglas Woods and Walter Gordon, Woods, Gordon & Co. had been

The Partners of
Clarkson, Gordon & Co.
request the pleasure of your company
at a Reception and Dinner
in celebration of the
100th Anniversary of the firm
on Thursday, September the seventeenth
nineteen hundred and sixty-four
The Royal York Hotel

Reception at 7.00 p.m.
Black Tie

R.S.V.P.

C. G.

Dinner

in celebration of

100th Anniversary

Clarkson, Gordon & Co.

The Royal York Hotel
Toronto, Ontario
Thursday, September 17th, 1964

Jack Wilson

established and nurtured into one of the most successful management consulting firms in the country. And thanks to the efforts of the Colonel, Walter Gordon, Grant Glassco and all the other partners, Clarkson, Gordon had been modernized and expanded into a national firm. Mr. Glassco had left the firm in 1957, and, with the retirement of Mr. Gordon, others were needed to lead the firm into its second century.

One such man was Jack Wilson. Mr. Wilson was born in Vancouver and lived in Kingston and Toronto before earning his degree in political science at the University of Toronto. In 1929, he was accepted as a student with the firm, partly on the basis of a recommendation from one of his professors, which stated: "Mr. Wilson is a man of good mental ability and, if he gets interested in your work, he will do well." How true this prediction turned out to be: he became a partner in 1941, he was appointed Chairman of the Management Committee (now called the Operations Policy Committee) in 1956, and in 1961 he became an Executive Partner. In 1963, he was nominated Chairman of the Executive Committee. Jack Wilson served the community and the profession in a variety of ways. From 1947 to 1950, he chaired the Accounting and Auditing Research Committee of the Canadian Institute of Chartered Accountants (CICA), and he served as President of the Institute of Chartered Accountants of Ontario (1956–7). A few years later, in 1966–7, he served as President of the CICA. Outside the firm, Mr. Wilson was a founding member and first Treasurer of the Lawrence Park Community Church, as well as President of the Canadian Red Cross Society, Ontario Division, 1963–4, and National President in 1971.

Jack Wilson was known and respected as a scholar and teacher, as well as an excellent accountant and shrewd businessman. Ron King, who had grown very close to him over the years, later recalled that his "strength was a combination of intelligence, a sense of humour and the ability to deal and talk with people."

His years of experience and his ability to work effectively with people gave him a true understanding of the firm's heritage and its potential. His intellect and his appreciation of the academic side of accounting tended to obscure the more humorous and pleasant side of his nature. To some, he projected the image of the teacher-professor, but to those who worked with him he was a warm individual – and one of the best accountants in the country.

There were other individuals who came into prominence in the firm in the two decades following the war. One was George Richardson, who earned his C.A. in 1926, joined the firm in 1927 and served as an Executive Partner from 1950 to 1969. In the 1950s, he played a major role in the development of Clarkson, Gordon's tax practice, and he influenced the careers of many of the younger partners, including Ross Skinner and Bill Farlinger, later key players in the firm. "George was simply unique," Harold Dixon recalled. "A very analytical mind. He could see his way through a problem better than anybody I ever knew. It was just a

George Richardson

privilege to work with him." His talents were considerable and often far-seeing. As a speaker said at his retirement dinner, "George was the first accountant in the world to publicly advocate deferred tax accounting."

George Richardson is remembered best for his two key characteristics: integrity and objectivity. "George was the model of what a professional should be," one senior partner later wrote. "His clients came first and nothing was permitted to interfere with the completion of an assignment. He had the ability of complete concentration of all his talents on the problem at hand."

One of George Richardson's closest associates was Ken Carr, who had joined the firm in 1939 and became a partner in 1951. For many years Mr. Carr handled the work for Massey Ferguson and, in the 1950s, he worked on a project for the Ontario Department of Highways. He gained a reputation in the profession for thoroughness and wise counsel. In 1972, he was made the first Chairman of the AYI Accounting and Auditing Advisory Committee, and two years later he became a member of the firm's Executive Committee, a position he held until 1979. He retired in 1981.

Alex Adamson was another partner who came to play an important role in the firm's post-war development. He joined Clarkson, Gordon in 1925, earned his C.A. in 1929 and became a partner in 1939. Mr. Adamson was a member of the Executive Committee during the pivotal period 1956–64 and took a great interest in building up the firm's art collection.

An equally towering figure was Arthur John "Pete" Little. Pete Little joined the firm in 1935 after graduating from the University of Western Ontario. He was made a partner in 1945 and remained with the firm for almost forty years, until his retirement in 1974. Mr. Little was "one of the best business developers in that period," one colleague remembered. "He had an amazing ability to remember names, and he was very active in the business community and charitable business organizations." Over the course of his career, Mr. Little held many important and prestigious positions, including President of the CICA, President of the Canadian Chamber of Commerce and President of the Toronto Board of Trade, Chairman of the Canadian Tax Foundation and a member of the Toronto General Hospital's Board of Trustees. After his retirement, Mr. Little joined the boards of directors of several major Canadian corporations.

Not only did these men make lasting contributions to the firm, several of their children also made their careers with Clarkson Gordon. For example, George Richardson had three sons who became partners: today Jay Richardson is a partner with Arthur

Arthur John "Pete" Little

Young International in Singapore; John Richardson is a senior officer with Trilon; and David Richardson is Chairman of Clarkson Gordon Inc. Pete Little's son, Peter, is a partner in the Toronto office; Dave Wilson, the son of Jack Wilson, came up through the London office and is now a partner in AY (U.S.) and is the National Director of Education for the American firm. A full list of children of partners who have served with the firm is too long to include;

suffice it to say that over the years it has been common for partners to send their children to Clarkson Gordon.

The firm also suffered its share of losses in the first few years after the centennial celebrations. In April 1966, Colonel Gordon died, after a long and distinguished career, and little more than a year later J.D. Woods passed away. Neither man was actively engaged in the affairs of the firm by this time, but with their deaths a link with the past was broken. A tribute to the Colonel in *Keeping Posted*, the firm's internal newsletter, could have been attributed to either man: "Undoubtedly, his two greatest loves were his family and his firm and he took great pride in the success and distinction that each achieved."

II

"As with all studies of history," Jack Wilson said in a speech at the annual Partners' Meeting on the eve of the one hundredth anniversary, "the value lies in finding out where we are today and providing a reasonable base for forecasting the future. One thing certainly runs through the history of this firm, and that is that conditions change – sometimes very quickly. And we have had to change to meet them. But it would be nonsense to think that this firm has changed because it has had to in order to survive. Our past history has been one of sensing what the changes may be and meeting them before they arrived."

There was a real sense that the firm and the business world were on the verge of great changes in the early 1960s. But there are always problems in understanding the past and seeing former events in historical perspective, especially when dealing with such a large partnership and practice. In this respect, however, Clarkson, Gordon is fortunate indeed, in being one of the few firms to have a portrait of the firm preserved in a magazine article so soon after its centennial.

Writing in *Globe Magazine* in May 1965, author and journalist Barbara Moon offered a "snapshot" of the firm. "There was a difference," the wife of one partner was quoted, "between being a chartered accountant and being a Clarkson man." But what was this difference? To the "connoisseur of the Canadian Establishment," Ms. Moon explained, Clarkson, Gordon & Co. was "the unofficial but effective finishing school – the only one in Canada aside from certain fashionable Toronto and Montreal law firms and investment houses – for young men of the Upper Class."

Ms. Moon went on to describe this process of "acculturation." Each year, a host of new students was brought into the firm at $400 to $500 per month to learn and gain first-hand experience. "By day, they work as juniors going on audits under the supervision of managers, each of whom in turn is supervised by a partner. By night, they study correspondence courses and complete written assignments for the Institute of Chartered Accountants . . . in between, the firm arranges its own lectures for them, including a course in public speaking."

Gradually, the new recruits would become acculturated – in matters of style and dress as well as professional conduct. The Colonel was "a stickler for form – and for a proper appearance," Ms. Moon explained. "A hat, for example, was *de rigueur*. Encountering a hatless employee at the entrance of the building on one occasion, the Colonel marched to the petty cash box, extracted a $10-bill and ordered the man to go and mend his appearance straightaway."

There were, of course, more important qualities for the younger members of the firm to emulate. Above all, there was recognition of the special relationship between the firm and its clients. As Ms. Moon described it: "An audit staff could do worse than line up outside the client's office for 10 minutes before starting work and just think about what they're there for; an accountant on a job should make it a point of pride to find one major saving for the client in the course of every audit; an accountant never opens his mouth about a client's affairs; a Clarkson man loses a client rather than sign a misleading financial statement; a Clarkson man is quietly self-confident; a Clarkson man is solicitous; a Clarkson man works nights, holidays and weekends, if a client needs him."

Students with potential emerged from each new class, and these few were groomed over subsequent years to assume greater responsibilities as managers and, eventually, partners. Before too long they had "the look". "No one has explicitly suggested to him the hat, the dark hose, the tab collar, the vest, the English wide-pant tailoring, the chaste cuff links, the garters. Somehow or other they just appear." What also appeared was the willingness to participate and contribute to the outside community. New partners were not obligated to give of their time and energy to charitable or community causes – they just did. And from their doing so, both the individual and the firm benefited.

The end result was a team of individuals, with each member of the firm having the freedom to innovate and develop his or her special talents to the fullest, while at the same time recognizing the unique tradition and importance of the firm as a whole. This mixture of individualism and teamwork had proved successful in the past, and in the 1960s it maintained Clarkson, Gordon as the leading firm in Canada and its partners as leaders in the profession.

Perhaps the Colonel put it best. At one point in his career, he was asked by the u.s. Securities and Exchange Commission for information on accounting principles in Canada. His reply was brief and very much to the point: "Accounting principles in Canada are what Clarkson, Gordon does."

III

For any business or firm to survive and prosper for 100 years is, in itself, a significant achievement and worthy of celebration. But a centennial also provides the opportunity for reflection – a chance to look back on the foundations of past success in order to prepare for future challenges. "The present partners," Jack Wilson wrote in 1964, "recognize the trust which has been imposed upon them ... and the need for never-ending vigilance to ensure that the standards [the founding partners] established are maintained and passed on untarnished to future generations."

In Mr. Wilson's view, the marking of a one hundredth birthday was, above all, a "time of challenge". "Our predecessors met many challenges in their time," he wrote, and in doing so they created a truly national firm. "We and our successors must be equally alert to the challenges of the future. We will have to adapt our skills, and where necessary, learn new skills to meet the changing needs of our clients and to ensure a satisfying professional life for the partners, managers, and staff which comprise the firm. Only if we do so can we be worthy of the first hundred years of the Clarkson, Gordon story."

CHAPTER EIGHT

On the Move

In the 1960s, anything seemed possible.
The Canadian economy was riding the crest of an unprecedented
boom that began with the end of the war and seemed as if it would
never end. Industry continued to expand and employment was
high as millions of Canadians rushed off to buy television sets,
refrigerators, automobiles and all manner of consumer goods. And
Canadians seemed ideally suited to make the most of the situation
– industrious and frugal as a people, politically stable and blessed
by geography and nature with unimaginable wealth in natural
resources above and below the ground.

The Canadian love affair with the mega-project continued: from
the St. Lawrence Seaway and TransCanada PipeLines of the 1950s
to the development of Churchill Falls, the Columbia River and
Manicouagan Dam in the 1960s. Canadians had the talent and
energy to provide the food and the fuel for an ever-shrinking and
increasingly hungry world. And this, it seemed, was only the
beginning.

The expansion of business throughout Canada had profound
implications for the firm. The birth of new businesses expanded
the pool of potential clients for Clarkson, Gordon, while the needs
of younger companies for experienced management consulting
services opened new doors of opportunity for Woods, Gordon. In
addition, many older clients that had come to the firm as small
companies had grown into vast corporations with operations across
the country and around the world. To serve these clients properly,

the expansion begun by the firm at the end of the war was continued through the 1960s.

One of the first areas to feel the surge in economic growth was Toronto. By the 1960s, Toronto was fast becoming the financial capital of Canada; indeed, it was one of the fastest-growing cities in the world. Its new vitality was expressed through the mixture of modern skyscrapers, high rises and parklands that transformed the cityscape and by the influx of people from around the world who recast Toronto into the multicultural and cosmopolitan metropolis that it is today.

In 1965, there was a total of 858 personnel in Clarkson, Gordon alone, of whom 75 were partners and 106 were managers. Of that total, 27 partners and 45 managers worked from the Toronto office. At the same time, 15 Wellington Street West, the building where most of the staff worked, had begun to show its age; the old building wheezed and creaked under the weight of a growing firm, and things began to break down. The boiler, for example, had been there for decades and would backfire and belch smoke with regularity. On one occasion, the smoke crept into the lower reception lobby and began spilling into adjacent offices. It became so thick that Ron King could hardly find his way to George Richardson's office. Once he got there, he found Mr. Richardson working away as if nothing was wrong. "George, aren't you worried about getting asphyxiated?" he asked. Mr. Richardson looked up, thought a moment and replied: "No, I think I'll be all right." Then he went back to work. That was the kind of man he was. That was the kind of trouble the building was in.

There was a great love for the building on Wellington Street – it was a beautiful and historic edifice that for half a century had been synonymous with the name Clarkson, Gordon. But something had to be done. The Clarkson Company and Woods, Gordon had expanded faster than anticipated, and no one had expected the tax practice to grow as rapidly as it had.

By 1967, the die had been cast. Negotiations were undertaken with The Toronto-Dominion Bank to sell the property on Wellington and move into the new Toronto-Dominion (T-D)

15 Wellington Street West

Centre a few blocks away. George Richardson and Duncan Gordon spearheaded the negotiations, and after all the details were checked and rechecked, an agreement was signed early in 1968.

The profits from the sale of 15 Wellington Street were divided equally among the partners of the firm. At that time there were participating and capital partners, and only the latter were actually entitled to a share of those profits. But Jack Wilson was determined that all partners be treated equally; Clarkson, Gordon was an egalitarian partnership in terms of opportunity and it was only fitting that all the partners share in the profits from the sale. The decision was welcomed by the partnership, and it served as another example of the special and equal relationship among Clarkson, Gordon partners.

The firm entered into a twenty-year lease with the T-D Centre

Above: View From Barrack Hill – Looking Down the Ottawa
Opposite: View From Barrack Hill / Ottawa River Canada
Selections from Wm. S. Hunter, Jr.'s *Hunter's Ottawa Scenery in the Vicinity of Ottawa City, Canada* are found in the Ottawa, Toronto, and Winnipeg offices.

for eight floors (twenty-fifth to thirty-second) in the Royal Trust Tower. The original plan was to occupy four immediately and expand into the other four as time went by. Woods, Gordon was assigned to the thirtieth floor, the Clarkson Company to a section on the twenty-ninth. Clarkson, Gordon would occupy the twenty-seventh, twenty-eighth and remaining sections on the twenty-ninth.

Responsibility for decorating the office fell to Alex Adamson, who in turn hired Robin Dyment of Eaton's to act as interior designer and help select the best possible furniture. One nice touch was the addition of the staircase between the twenty-seventh and twenty-eighth floors, a replica of a staircase in the Seagram

76

building in New York. Both the T-D Centre and the Seagram building were designed by Mies Van der Rohe, and Mr. Adamson and Ms. Dyment believed that this distinctive staircase would add a special flavour to the office.

One unusual problem emerged concerning the firm's growing art collection. Under Grant Glassco's direction, the firm had begun collecting Canadian prints, and after he retired the responsibility fell to Mr. Adamson. For years, Mr. Adamson had visited galleries in Toronto, Montreal and New York to buy prints and, by the time of the move, the collection had grown to between 800 and 900 pieces. The collection consisted of Canadian prints ranging from the historical to the contemporary, from individual pieces to whole series by various artists, and included the best collection of W.H. Bartlett prints in the country. By the mid-1960s it was more than merely art-work on the office walls, it was one of the finest collections of Canadian prints in the world.

The job of moving the print collection to the T-D Centre was no easy task. Mr. Adamson also concluded that, while many of the original frames were beautiful, as a group they lacked consistency and would not be suitable for the new environs. He decided that all the prints would be rematted and reframed before being moved. The end result was an art collection that reflected the more modern appearance of the firm while preserving the integrity of the individual prints. And perhaps as a symbolic gesture, Mr. Adamson bought a number of more contemporary prints once the firm had moved into its new premises.

The collection continued to grow and, in 1988, numbered about three thousand pieces in the Toronto office alone. Today, responsibility for the art collection is in the capable hands of David Richardson, Chairman of Clarkson Gordon Inc. Many of the more valuable prints could easily have become museum pieces, but thanks to the efforts of Grant Glassco, Alex Adamson and David Richardson, a unique assortment of Canadian prints can be seen today in offices from coast to coast.

Final preparations for the move were made over the summer and autumn of 1969, and the new office officially opened on November 1. While there was great sadness in leaving Wellington Street, there was also the recognition that the decision to move was a wise one. The new arrangements suited the needs of the firm, and additional space could be acquired when necessary. Besides, as Mr. Wilson pointed out in 1971, there were more important things to Clarkson, Gordon than any one building: "Premises, clients and type of practice are all parts of the history of a firm or an office, but the most important element in our growth and development has been, and will continue to be, the people – partners, managers and staff – who have made up the firm."

II

The process, begun at the end of the war, to expand Clarkson, Gordon on a national basis into a strong player in the market-places important to the firm's long-term stability continued in the 1960s. Ottawa was a prime target; the growth of the federal government's role in the social and economic sectors offered potential business through Crown corporation audit appointments and in the taxation area. To meet this potential, an office was opened in Ottawa in 1965 by Fred Mallett. From modest beginnings, with one partner, one manager, and a total staff of five, the Ottawa practice expanded rapidly in the late 1960s. In 1969, it merged with the firm Milne, Honeywell and Burpee, a respected regional practice with offices in Renfrew as well as Ottawa. The Ottawa office has prospered under the leadership of John Morrison, Henry Pankratz, Stu Sutcliffe and, more recently, such senior partners as Wayne Penny and Steve Gallagher, the current Office Managing Partner.

A second major area of growth in the 1960s was in the Maritimes. In the spring of 1965, an office was opened in Halifax, not through a merger with a local firm but through the efforts of Bob Cameron, who had been sent there from the Toronto office. At first the Halifax office's role was to undertake the work of existing clients, but gradually new clients were found. In 1968, the office began to carry on insolvency work after Rod McCulloch was transferred there to become the audit manager. By the 1980s, the Halifax office had established itself, with such major locally based national clients as National Sea Products, Maritime Tel and Tel and Newfoundland Capital Corporation. Today it has a total staff of over 40, including 5 partners and 9 managers. In 1986, Rod McCulloch left the firm to join National Sea Products, and the office has since been led by Paul Campbell.

The year after the Halifax practice began, negotiations were undertaken with the Saint John, New Brunswick firm Cox & Hammett, leading to a merger with Clarkson, Gordon effective May 1, 1967. Tom Hammett, who had been with Clarkson, Gordon in the early 1930s, became the first partner in the new office, and in 1968 he was joined by Steve Lowden as Office Managing Partner. The Saint John practice grew over subsequent years, along with many of its clients – for example, New Brunswick Telephone Company, Limited (NB Tel) – and has a clientele of large and small New Brunswick businesses. The office was involved in a number of important projects during these years, including the bankruptcy of Bricklin Motors Ltd. By 1978, the firm had expanded to such an extent that new quarters were acquired in the Brunswick Square office tower in Saint John. In 1970, Rollie Lutes, a New Brunswicker by birth, moved back to Saint John as Office Managing Partner. He was responsible for the success of the practice until 1985, when Keith Bowman became the new Office Managing Partner.

In each of the new offices, the partners and managers participated in the local community – on the Board of Trade and Chamber of Commerce and in the United Way, the YMCA and many other organizations and local charities. Whether the new office opened as a result of a merger or through the work of newcomers, all partners and managers in Clarkson, Gordon were expected to maintain the high standards established by the firm.

III

In 1967, Canada celebrated its centennial (as Clarkson, Gordon had done only three years earlier), and the occasion was marked in thousands of ways in hundreds of communities all across Canada. Every city, town and village took on some special centennial project, from restoration of a historic building, to publication of a commemorative history, to opening a new community centre. The biggest celebration of all was Montreal's Expo '67, a triumphant world's fair in which more than sixty nations participated. Part of the art collection of the Montreal office was displayed in the Canadian Pavilion. The themes – Man the Explorer, Man the Producer, Man the Creator and Man in the Community – the mood and the architecture seemed to herald the dawn of a new age, of space travel and computers.

The technological age had already arrived at Clarkson, Gordon and Woods, Gordon. One true pioneer in the field of computers, and the founder of Woods, Gordon's computer consulting practice, was David Watson, a graduate of the London School of Economics, who joined the firm in 1949. He brought with him a wealth of experience as a systems analyst with Univac Canada and during the late 1950s and the 1960s helped move the firm into a position of leadership in computer consulting with such work as his pioneering studies with the Toronto Stock Exchange and his editorship of the Computer Society of Canada's annual "Census of Computers".

On the accounting and auditing side, the groundwork for the current National Department structure was laid by Jack Wilson. Mr. Wilson, because of his interests and erudition, was the partner of choice for second opinions when difficult accounting and auditing matters arose. As the firm grew, and demand broadened, "Jack latched on to Ross Skinner as someone else who was equally interested in accounting and theoretical discussion," in the words of Ken Carr. Responsibility for research and technical guidance fell to Mr. Skinner, who had become a partner in 1954 and gradually assumed the role of "resident academic."

Two other "big-picture" people caught Jack Wilson's eye. One was David Lay, who had joined the firm in 1952. The other was Rod Anderson, who had joined the firm in 1956, after a conversation with his neighbour – Jack Wilson. Mr. Lay's and Mr. Anderson's paths crossed a lot after that – "often," a current partner remembers, "in the form of vigorous and entertaining arguments with each other over professional issues as members of the firm's Accounting and Auditing Policy Committee."

David Lay, while working closely with the two original National Departments (Accounting and Auditing), never did belong to one of them. By the late 1980s, however, when he assumed his role as Vice-Chairman of the firm, he also took on responsibility for professional practice and as the person to whom all the associated National Directors reported. Rod Anderson, on the other hand, was part of the "national" initiative from the beginning. A rather modest beginning at that: John Kirkwood, a long-time partner in the National Accounting group, recalled that "Ross Skinner and Jack Wilson had talked for some time about establishing a formal national function to provide consultation on accounting and auditing matters, and 'took the plunge' in 1962 to commit one C.A. as a full-time researcher and adviser." At the same time, Ross Skinner built an experimental staff, which combined audit and research work.

From that beginning, the National Accounting and National Auditing departments have grown. From those precedents, the departments have established an enviable reputation in the profession as the premier research and development group, leading the way in the development of methodology, standard-setting and quality assurance. Many of the National Directors have done their "tour of duty" and gone on to other major roles in the firm, including Ron Gage and Bob Long. The present National Directors, Bob Lord in Accounting and David Selley in Auditing, continue to maintain the performance levels set by their predecessors.

These national departments, and those that followed in other areas, provided the basis for a national professional practice with consistent standards and extensive consultative support for accounting and auditing problems identified by the firm's practitioners.

From the start, they also carried a share of client responsibilities themselves. A continuing theme was the extensive work done with prospectuses, which remains a major activity today. All of the reasons for creating the "National" structure may not stand out, but Don Scott suspects that one of the clues to establishing when the need for the structure was identified was when there was a policy decision that all prospectuses being developed require a second review.

Consultation and client service kept the national group busy, but it did not counteract the commitment to research and development. Significant resources were devoted to ensuring that the firm would continue to be one of the most innovative in the profession.

Innovation came from many directions, but one pair of contributors stood out. From their earliest days together, Ross Skinner and Rod Anderson teamed up and, widely identified as "Skinner and Anderson", became perhaps the second-best-known

Ross Skinner

duo in the firm to the outside world – after "Clarkson and Gordon", of course.

Together, Ross Skinner and Rod Anderson embarked on a research project that led to the development of a systems-oriented approach to auditing, what they called analytical auditing – "a change in our approach to the evidence we were gathering," Mr. Skinner recalled, "with greater reliance on the client's systems for processing and recording transactions, rather than detailed checking one by one. Analytical auditing was merely a technique by flow charts, attaining a grasp of what the client's system was, so that you could then evaluate its strengths and weaknesses and you could concentrate on the weaknesses in your audit procedures."

The fruits of their labours were published in 1966 under the title *Analytical Auditing*. This book was only the beginning of a longer project, but it enjoyed enormous success from the very start. Within a few years, it had been translated into half a dozen languages and had become standard reading in the profession. In the mid-1970s, their work was extended through the publication of *The External Audit*, which incorporated analytical auditing techniques with newer material on computer auditing and statistical sampling. *The External Audit* was, and continues to be, the only auditing text written wholly in Canada and based on Canadian experience.

By the time *The External Audit* was published, Clarkson, Gordon was already the leader in computer auditing. The first computer in Canada was owned by the University of Toronto, and consisted of "two rooms full of radio tubes," Rod Anderson recalled. "And you had to feed it all in zeros and ones." Beginning with punch-card systems and electronic calculators, Mr. Anderson and Bill MacDonald, the partner he worked for at the time, were introduced to the new world of computer technology.

Some of the firm's larger clients, like BP Oil and Confederation Life, had already acquired computers, and it was clear that the new technology would have a great effect on the future of auditing. Rod Anderson participated in the CICA's task force on computers and spearheaded the development of Clarkson, Gordon's computer training program. It was an enormous task. Before members of the staff could learn the methods of computer auditing they had to learn something about computers, and this meant that two courses would be required – one as a basic introduction to computers, the other to teach computer auditing.

The next question was how to reach all the members of the firm. The answer was a novel one: through the use of video training films. "In our naïveté," Mr. Anderson remembered, "we thought television stations would know something about producing educational television." As it turned out, the venture was as new to the television people as it was to the firm. Clarkson, Gordon's first Computer Concepts course was filmed in 1967, in the studios of the Toronto station CFTO. Conditions were rather primitive, especially in the production of graphics: "We had these big grey boards," Mr. Anderson explained, "and two guys, with cans on their heads, listening to the control room, would hold the big grey board and lower it one line at a time."

In the end, the project was a tremendous success. The CICA was given the use of the course, and it was used throughout the Canadian profession. Moreover, the American and British institutes also took it, making Clarkson, Gordon one of the international leaders in video training. The following year, 1968, the firm installed its own computer (IBM System 36) for internal administration purposes. The team of individuals who worked on the project was the start of what eventually became Clarkson, Gordon's computer audit specialist group.

The rise of computer technology was only one aspect of the changing financial and business environment in the late 1960s. The push for higher and higher standards in accounting meant that the need for research and innovation would likely increase. The increasing concentration of industry in huge multinational corporations had made it more difficult for smaller firms to serve their clients or keep up on research. The rising internationalization of business also produced the need for closer relations with the firm's fellow members in Arthur Young International. Not only were Canadian corporations spreading abroad, but foreign companies (especially those based in the English-speaking world) were increasingly insisting that their audits in Canada be done by their international affiliates. This led to a certain rationalization within the profession, with the loss of some large international clients and the gaining of others through Arthur Young.

In 1970, the Management Committee addressed many of these concerns in a lengthy memorandum examining the future of the firm. It noted "a world trend towards increasing the size of corporations and a greater concentration of management control. This can have considerable effect on our practice. Companies which are important to us as clients may be relatively unimportant to the parent company or its auditors." In addition, the memorandum continued, as "companies get larger, it becomes necessary to assign greater resources at the partner and manager level. The audit partners and managers will have to devote a larger proportion of their time to a smaller number of large clients."

Further, the growing diversification of these clients would inevitably produce greater specialization within the firm in order to deal better with their specific needs.

The Management Committee's memorandum was studied at the 1970 Partners' Meeting, with a view to preparing the firm for the next ten to fifteen years. It was agreed that the accounting and auditing standards groups would need to be enhanced if Clarkson, Gordon were to maintain its position of leadership in the profession. The increasingly complex taxation field was singled out as an area for further specialization, and there was some discussion of the idea of assigning a tax partner to each large client. In the international arena, it was agreed to strengthen relations with the member firms of Arthur Young International, but not at the expense of the firm's Canadian identity. Above all, it was recognized that for the firm to maintain its success it must continue to recruit new men and women of the very highest quality. But these decisions did not signify a break with the past; they were more a recognition that no firm — however successful — could stand still to meet the challenges of a new decade.

CHAPTER NINE

Notre
visage français

"THE QUEBEC GOVERNMENT'S burst of interventionism and entrepreneurship during the Jean Lesage administration of the early 1960s was not unique," wrote historian Michael Bliss in his book *Northern Enterprise*. "The difference in Quebec was that the Lesage government quickly identified its policies with the advancement of Canada's second-largest ethnic group. While other governments talked vaguely about serving all the people, the Quebec government set out to be the agent for elevating French Canadians in Quebec life and in Canada." Beginning in 1960, the Quebec government embarked on a vast program of development in areas as diverse as hydro-electricity, the steel industry, pension plans and investment projects. New doors were opened for French-Canadian entrepreneurs, and thousands of young Quebeckers flooded into the burgeoning business schools.

For Clarkson, Gordon, the Quiet Revolution posed a challenge. The Montreal office had been opened as early as 1922, but the staff was almost exclusively English-speaking, as were its clients. Could the process of post-war expansion be broadened to include a French-speaking practice? It would take time for the answer to that question to become clear – years of facing new challenges and discovering new opportunities.

I

To understand the growth of the Montreal office and the birth of Clarkson, Gordon's French-speaking practice, one must begin with Marcel Caron. A native of Montreal, Mr. Caron studied at

Marcel Caron

l'École des Hautes Études Commerciales de Montréal. During his years as a student, he worked on the student newspaper and supported himself by working during the evenings as a clerk for the City of Montreal. Shortly after his graduation in 1943, he joined Clarkson, Gordon. Mr. Caron later explained how his association with Clarkson, Gordon began: "I had received offers from five other firms, but the manager of the [Montreal] office in those days was a chap called Bud Wait, and there seemed to be some chemistry between him and myself. So, he hired me at ten dollars less than someone else was offering me. But I had confidence in the guy, and we had a good interview."

When Mr. Caron joined the firm, there were no francophone

partners and he was the sole French-speaking student. The office, moreover, primarily serviced the branch offices of Toronto clients. Walter Gordon, who was determined to enlarge the francophone side of the practice, saw great potential in Mr. Caron. In 1945, after Mr. Caron passed his C.A. exams (for which he won the Valiquette prize as highest-ranking French student), Walter Gordon invited him to Toronto for further training. Most of the next two years was spent in Toronto, where Mr. Caron worked for Pete Little and Lawson Sherring. At first it was tough – "after three months I started dreaming in English," Mr. Caron recalled – but it was a tremendous learning experience.

In 1947, Mr. Caron returned to Montreal as a manager, and in 1949 he was invited to become a partner. His years in Toronto had introduced him to important aspects of the national firm. It had also produced many lifelong friendships. "I could phone them up," he later reflected. "I knew who they were. They knew who I was. We could exchange ideas. We were friends. And they also took a great interest in the work that I wanted to develop."

Upon his return to Montreal, Mr. Caron began to put his ideas into operation. His first act was to hire a bilingual receptionist and a bilingual secretary; this was "the beginning," he explained, "of a movement to make the Quebec practice fully bilingual." But it was slow-going at first. Mr. Caron shared responsibility for the Montreal office with Don Parkinson, and the two men were still "young rookies" who were hard-pressed to say that they had "all the experience or the prestige in the community that one needed in those days to succeed."

The first task was to assemble a solid and capable staff. Fortune smiled on the Montreal office in the 1950s when Arthur Gilmour left his post in the Department of National Revenue to join the firm. Mr. Gilmour had an outstanding reputation as a tax specialist; indeed, his writings on taxation became standard reading for a generation of students, tax practitioners, law firms and tax specialists in industry. Arriving at the Montreal office, he was met by Messrs. Caron and Parkinson who sat down and said: "You're well known, you're experienced, you're well respected – pick out the best office."

Arthur Gilmour

Under Mr. Gilmour's direction, a large tax practice was developed in the Montreal office. Everyone benefited from the presence of Arthur Gilmour, Mr. Caron recalled, "because he directed us, he trained us, he corrected us. And being in his shadow, we were known to be good on taxes." Mr. Gilmour's presence also attracted important clients to the firm.

Another important addition was George Keeping. Mr. Keeping was with another firm in Montreal, and, after being transferred to Toronto, he became involved in the audit of a company in which Walter Gordon had an interest. The story was told that he fought

George Keeping

hard with Mr. Gordon on a particular matter and finally swayed him round to his opinion ("as a good auditor would," said Mr. Caron). Mr. Gordon was impressed, and he asked Mr. Keeping to join Clarkson, Gordon. Mr. Keeping agreed, on condition that he be allowed to practise in Montreal. Mr. Keeping made such an important contribution to the firm that it has been rumoured that the name of the firm's newsletter, *Keeping Posted*, was more than mere coincidence.

Within a few years Don Parkinson had returned to Toronto, leaving the trio of Caron, Gilmour and Keeping as the partners responsible for the Montreal office. For Mr. Caron, the prime concern was to attract local business to the firm; only this way, he believed, would he be able to build up a French-speaking clientele. And to attract local business, he pointed out, "we had to get the name of our firm known. We were well-known on the English side – we were unknown on the French side. And I knew it would be a long road to get the name known and accepted."

Mr. Caron became actively involved in the Chamber of Commerce in Montreal and made many contacts there and through the dozens of other community activities in which he participated. He also began lecturing at l'École des Hautes Études, which exposed him to the rising generation of francophone business students and gave him a unique opportunity to spot talented young students for the firm. In this way he handpicked a French-speaking staff, one by one, beginning with Jérome Carrière.

Mr. Carrière developed into one of Mr. Caron's closest associates and a leader in the accounting profession. He distinguished himself, by both his devotion and his competence, in many activities of public interest. He created the firm's linguistic services group, now working in six different languages. He became President of the Ordre des comptables agréés du Québec and for eleven years acted as Treasurer of the *Revue Commerce*, a leading francophone business magazine. His untimely death in 1981 left a great void in the firm. A prestigious journalism award was created in his memory.

Gradually, the Montreal office began acquiring local clients. The first major French-speaking client was *La Presse*, Montreal's largest newspaper. The company was large and influential but was experiencing a very difficult financial period. Mr. Caron and his team set to work to help rebuild *La Presse*, and the prestigious newspaper has remained a client ever since.

The relationship with *La Presse* also led to other projects. At one point in his work on the newspaper, Mr. Caron needed the co-operation of the Quebec government. He telephoned Walter Gordon, who suggested that he go directly to Jean Lesage, who had become Premier in 1960.

"Lesage won't even look at me," Mr. Caron told Mr. Gordon, to which the latter replied: "Well, maybe he will look at me. How about if I go with you?"

Walter Gordon was an old and trusted friend of Premier Lesage, and he accompanied Mr. Caron to Quebec City. After almost an hour of conversation, in which the problem concerning *La Presse* was resolved, Premier Lesage asked if Clarkson, Gordon would be interested in assuming the audit of Hydro-Québec. The unification of all the private electric companies into Hydro-Québec was the largest and most famous project undertaken by the government of Jean Lesage; it was synonymous with the Quiet Revolution, and it symbolized the rise of a francophone entrepreneurial business class.

Thus began a relationship with Hydro-Québec that was to last for a quarter-century. The impact on the firm was enormous: "Being auditor of Hydro-Québec really put us on the map in Quebec," Mr. Caron explained. "People got to know about Clarkson, Gordon and got to know about our influence." This was a period of tremendous growth and development for Hydro-Québec. The firm's experience in public financing, in both the Canadian and the U.S. markets, proved a very important factor for what was to become one of the major public utilities in North America.

The Montreal office was gaining momentum as other clients were attracted to the firm. It was also gaining a reputation in the universities. Denis Desautels, current Office Managing Partner of the Montreal office, recalled his reasons for joining Clarkson, Gordon in 1964 as a young student from McGill: "At that time, it was a relatively small office, but one that was seen to have a reputation on campus of being a very fast-growing practice. I was discouraged at the time by most of the students at McGill University from joining Clarkson, Gordon because they were extremely busy and people were working enormous amounts of overtime. If you went with some of their competitors, you hardly worked any overtime and went into a nice, easy articling period."

93

In addition to the potential that Clarkson, Gordon offered, Mr. Desautels noted, "among the national firms, it had the best identity within the French business community."

The Montreal office was, until 1962, the firm's only office in Quebec. In that year, the firm achieved a long-cherished ambition when it opened an office in Quebec City and then, a few months later, entered into a merger with DeCoster, Normandeau & Cie. At the time of the merger, Maurice DeCoster retired to look after personal business interests and Raymond Normandeau became a partner in Clarkson, Gordon. It was an important decision, Gérard Limoges, Executive Partner for the Quebec region, later reflected: "À ce moment-là, nous étions au début de la révolution tranquille et il est alors apparu opportun de présenter au Québec notre visage français étant donné que Clarkson, Gordon était à peu près le seul cabinet national à avoir admis à l'époque des canadiens-français dans les rangs d'associés." (At that time, we were on the verge of the Quiet Revolution, and we saw an opportunity to present our French image to Quebec, as Clarkson Gordon was essentially the only national firm to welcome French Canadians to the partnership.)

II

The winds of change continued to blow in Quebec throughout the 1960s. "We could tell that the centre of influence was changing in Quebec," Mr. Caron explained. "We could see pools of capital being accumulated, like the *caisses populaires*, and made real efforts to have an influence on those pools of capital." Through contacts in the Chamber of Commerce and in the community, and because of the firm's reputation in the tax field, the Montreal office was able to build up a wealth of francophone clients.

Mr. Caron's relationship with Premier Lesage became closer over the following years. "The Premier would consult with me. He would call me once or twice a month and ask my advice on things he wanted to do and people he wanted to hire," said Mr. Caron, and this in turn led to more government assignments from Quebec City. The number of public activities increased as well for Mr.

Caron. In 1962, he sat on the board that prepared the ground for the Société générale de financement, a provincial corporation created to foster the growth of Quebec businesses. In 1967, he was asked to chair a committee established by the Chamber of Commerce of Quebec to investigate the economic effects of three alternatives: federalism, sovereignty-association and independence. Later, he became a trustee of Montreal's Notre-Dame Church, a founding member of the Canada Committee, and President of the Opéra du Québec.

The election victory of Daniel Johnson and the Union nationale in 1966 reflected the changes taking place in Quebec and, inevitably, affected the way in which the Montreal office conducted its business. Mr. Caron knew the new premier from their days at l'École des Hautes Études, when both wrote for the campus newspaper (another contributor at the time had been a young law student named Pierre Elliott Trudeau). After his victory, Premier Johnson telephoned Mr. Caron from Quebec City.

He indicated that, although he was pleased with Clarkson, Gordon's work on Hydro-Québec, the climate of the times had led the government to feel that a firm with a French name was needed to act as auditors. "More and more," Mr. Desautels explained, "the economy was being taken in hand by the French-speaking population, and they, as well as the government on the whole at that time, expressed a clear preference for dealing with a firm with a French name, and even though the people would be the same, it became, for many, a matter of principle." The government of Quebec was satisfied with the work of Clarkson, Gordon and had no wish to cut its ties with the firm. The solution was to have Mr. Caron act as auditor personally and to sign all the statements "Marcel Caron, partner of Clarkson, Gordon of Montreal".

This new arrangement worked satisfactorily for several years but gradually became something of a nuisance for Mr. Caron. Having been appointed personally meant that he had to be there to sign all documents, large or small — he could not give a proxy. "I had to be present every time there was a financing in New York," he recalled, "and sometimes, to my great displeasure, there was an air

95

strike. Once I happened to be in France and I had to fly back to New York to be there to sign the papers." And what would happen if he got sick? "I couldn't let them miss a $300-million issue, so sick or not, I would have to go to New York."

Eventually this problem was sorted out. In the early 1970s, a new partnership was created – H. Marcel Caron & Associés – consisting of all the Clarkson, Gordon partners in Quebec. This way, any partner could sign for Mr. Caron on behalf of the firm. The new partnership was registered and operated under that name and collected fees, but it made no profit and did not have a separate account from Clarkson, Gordon. In a sense, it was a parallel arrangement within which all the partners moved freely.

By the mid-1970s, the Montreal practice was well established in the Quebec business community. Although part of a national organization, it had special responsibility for the handling of francophone clients and in this respect had to be self-sufficient. But self-reliance was never pursued at the expense of the national organization; if anything, the interdependence of the offices increased as the needs of clients expanded on a national scale. And when it came to standards of accounting and auditing there was only one level – the very highest.

Over the years the Montreal office has benefited from the strong leadership of several Office Managing Partners, including Don Scott, Bill Farlinger, John Morrison, Gérard Limoges and Denis Desautels. In addition, senior partners such as Chuck Bissegger, Guy Chamberland and Ron Pearl have made significant contributions to the growth and success of the Montreal office.

In July 1988, the Montreal office moved from its twenty-year tenure on Dorchester Boulevard (now Boulevard René-Lévesque) to Place Ville Marie, a landmark in Montreal.

III

Perhaps the greatest satisfaction for the partners and staff in the Montreal office comes from being able to participate in the growth and development of francophone businesses as they grow from small family operations into large companies in the national and international arenas. The ability to work with all sizes of companies has always been a strength of the firm; indeed, Clarkson Gordon takes great pride in its owner-operator practice, which has demonstrated on many occasions what the firm can do to help small companies develop into major corporations. Provigo Inc. is a good example. Provigo became a client in 1961, with total sales of approximately $9 million. The firm and the company grew together over the following years. As the company broadened and diversified its operations, the firm responded with more specialized services, particularly in the financial and tax areas. A regional report in the fall of 1987 described it this way: "We helped the company go public in 1962; have assisted with a number of mergers and acquisitions through the years; and have provided almost every special service conceivable." And the efforts have paid off – by 1987, Provigo's sales volume had risen to the $6-billion range.

There are other examples, too. Another client that came in the 1960s was Telemedia – a small communications company that has grown into a giant in the field. And there was Repap Enterprises, which began as an idea from George Petty in the 1970s and has developed into "one of the country's most dynamic paper makers". Everybody wins from this kind of growth; good work by the firm helps companies grow, and this in turn produces greater revenue for the firm, enhances its reputation in the community and attracts new clients. "We can say that many of our clients have relied on our firm for a lot of assistance," Mr. Limoges pointed out. "We have provided first-class service and derived many benefits."

CHAPTER TEN

Here Come
the Seventies

To a traveller who had been out of the country for twenty-five years after 1945, the firm he or she would have found on returning in 1970 would have been virtually unrecognizable. Statistics never tell the whole truth, but they can be instructive. In 1971, the firm consisted of 162 partners, 203 managers and a total staff of 1,618, spread out in offices from coast to coast. Indeed, the firm had more than doubled in size in less than ten years. The Ontario base was solid; in Quebec a new partnership had been created and the practice was flourishing; and in the west and in the Maritimes, new offices had been opened and steady progress was being made. But there was also a negative side to such rapid growth: for the first time, it was becoming impossible for partners to know all their colleagues in the national firm and, in some cases, even in their own office.

An important change occurred on March 1, 1971, when Duncan Lockhart Gordon assumed the role of Chairman of the Executive Committee. If only as the son of the Colonel and the brother of Walter Gordon, Duncan Gordon would have been well known and respected in the firm; but Duncan Gordon was very much his own man. Following a distinguished military service during the Second World War (for which he was made a Member of the Order of the British Empire – M.B.E.), Mr. Gordon joined the firm and took an active part in its national expansion. He was well respected and admired in the profession and in 1963 served as President of the Institute of Chartered Accountants of Ontario.

Duncan Gordon was a strong, straight-thinking man, who was

accustomed to getting his way but willing to change if his ways were proved wrong. Many present-day partners look back fondly on their years with Duncan Gordon. Mr. Gordon held a strong belief in "management by walking around". He was a strong proponent of being visible, available to assist and support his partners. "One of the very significant factors that really affected my career was the opportunity I had to work closely with Duncan Gordon," reflected David Lay, today the Vice-Chairman of the Executive Committee. "I'm sure that would be true of many partners in the firm. They would relate to Duncan who, despite his façade of being somewhat distant and gruff, was a very warm human being. He was a great 'people person'. And the real strength that Duncan displayed was the ability to let other people take the credit. Invariably, Duncan was behind the scenes, advising and counselling other partners."

Mr. Gordon never became actively involved in politics, but he shared Walter Gordon's commitment to economic justice and the growth of a strong and independent Canada. He never married, and those who were close to him knew that there were two special loves in his life: the firm and the Hospital for Sick Children. Mr. Gordon's involvement with the hospital spanned almost as many years as he was with the firm and included a dozen years as Chairman of its Board. His work for the hospital was recognized in 1987 when he was awarded the Order of Ontario. As for the firm, Mr. Gordon thrived on the challenge and the excitement. "What is really stimulating," he recalled in *Keeping Posted*, "is to come down here every morning, knowing that something unexpected will happen. As senior partner you are involved in everything. Whenever anything exciting happens, or there is a crisis, people phone you."

II

Of all the developments in Clarkson, Gordon during the 1970s, perhaps the most significant was the evolution of the tax practice into a major contributor to the overall growth and success of the firm. The development of a strong tax practice, however, was not a

Duncan Gordon (Photo: Ashley-Crippen)

phenomenon of the 1970s alone – its roots stretched back to the years following the Second World War. The growing complexity of the tax system, coupled with increasing rates of taxation in the post-war era, provided fertile soil for the growth of a specialized tax practice.

In 1953, Clarkson, Gordon's small tax practice was based in Toronto and Montreal. In Montreal, as we have seen, the growth and development of the tax practice were spearheaded by Arthur Gilmour. In Toronto, the emerging tax group was headed by George Richardson and Pete Little. The 1948 tax act and the 1952 consolidation brought more precise rules, and these two men gradually came to devote more and more time to the area. Growth during the 1950s was relatively slow, but by 1962 there were three additional tax partners in the Toronto office: Ralph Dilworth, Kerr Gibson and Eric Ford. David Lay, then a manager, joined the group for a short time when transferred from Hamilton in 1961. Glen Cronkwright moved in from London in a similar capacity in 1962 to gain experience – a two-year transfer that expanded to twenty.

By 1965, there were 21 tax specialists (7 partners, 9 managers and 5 staff) nationally, 12 of whom were in the Toronto office. To deal more effectively with the growing national tax practice, a group of tax specialists was transferred from the Toronto practice office and formed the National Tax Group. The new group was headed by Eric Ford, the firm's first National Tax Director. Glen Cronkwright took over leadership of the Toronto practice. The National Tax Group does not directly focus on client work – its role is to look after national issues such as quality control, client tax memoranda, internal information dissemination and staff training. Today, the Group comprises more than a dozen individuals, and it continues to function independently of the Toronto office.

A new round of tax reform began in the late 1960s, beginning with the 1967 Report of the Carter Royal Commission, which, after some five years of study, recommended very radical changes to the tax system. Many of these proposals were studied and modified by the government over the following years, culminating in the tax act of 1971. Responding to the new challenge, the firm's tax partners gathered together to produce a series of three booklets on the proposed changes: the first dealt with the government's proposals, the second with the work and views of the Commons and the Senate committees set up to review the government's tax reform proposals, and the third, produced in 1971, with the changes introduced to the tax system (including the introduction of Canada's first tax on capital gains). The latter booklet, entitled *Tomorrow's Taxes*, was published for use by Clarkson, Gordon staff and clients. Sixteen thousand copies were printed at first, and the

CICA also published it (with a different cover) for use across the country. It was a mammoth task, but thanks to the hard work of many staff members, *Tomorrow's Taxes* became the standard work on the new tax act.

Production of memoranda on tax issues, proposals and amendments, for the benefit of both clients and staff, has been a tradition of the firm's tax practice for many years. Probably the first significant venture into tax publications was the production – now a regular feature – of a budget letter commentary immediately following the budget presentation by the Minister of Finance. This is produced by a writing team centred in Toronto and printed overnight and distributed to all offices for delivery early next morning to clients from coast to coast.

The first few efforts, while of great interest to the firm's clients and staff, received no exposure in the press. This changed dramatically following the federal budget of June 13, 1963. Hansard quotes the interchange between the Honourable D.H. Harkness, Conservative member for Calgary North, and the Honourable Walter L. Gordon, Minister of Finance. Mr. Harkness stated:

Mr. Speaker, I rise on a question of privilege affecting the entire house. On Friday morning, June 14, there was delivered to a Calgary law office at 9.30 a.m., by the first morning mail delivery, a memorandum entitled "Proposed Changes in Canadian Taxes". The memorandum summarizes the budget, has a budget resolutions index and attached to it are appendices containing the budget resolutions. The whole runs to 25 pages and is under a covering letter from Clarkson, Gordon and Company of Toronto. The envelope containing this material is metered, and the meter stamp bears the date of June 14.

The question which arises is how this material could have been prepared multi-graphed and delivered by ordinary mail to a Calgary office by 9.30 a.m. on Friday after the budget was presented here on Thursday evening. It may be possible that this analysis of the budget could have been prepared, the material mimeographed and the

whole dispatched to Calgary, and I presume to every other city in
Canada, and then delivered within the times I have given. However, it
seems somewhat improbable.

Walter Gordon answered the attack later that day:

I have just received a telegram from Mr. J.R.M. Wilson, who is the
senior partner of Clarkson, Gordon and Company, chartered accountants. The telegram reads as follows:

"Budget address and resolutions released by Bank of Canada Toronto
to interested parties starting about nine twenty eastern daylight
time. We received two copies at nine forty five June 13 and two copies
at nine fifty five. On receipt of these our partners reviewed the
speech and resolutions and prepared an explanatory memorandum
which was typed and multi-lithed. Concurrently copies of the resolu-
tion were photocopied and a copy of these together with the explanatory memorandum were mailed to clients of the firm in pre-addressed
envelopes together with a covering letter dated June 13 which had
also been prepared in advance after the date of the budget had been
announced. First completed memoranda were ready by twelve midnight and first mailing left our office at one fifteen eastern daylight
time and delivered to the Malton post office in time to catch flight
No. 501 which stops at Winnipeg, Regina, Calgary and Vancouver,
leaving Toronto at two fifty a.m. eastern daylight time. This flight
due in Calgary at six twenty a.m. mountain standard time. Procedure
followed by our firm was consistent in every respect with that
followed for the past several years."

Two primary components of the tax practice are support for the
audit practice in its review of client tax accruals, as part of the
regular audit work, and completion of tax returns – for individuals
as well as corporations – Canadians and non-Canadians alike.
Perhaps the most exciting area, however, and the area in which
most specialist tax partners and managers spend much of their
time, can be found in tax planning: anticipating and advising on

104

structuring transactions for businesses and ensuring that clients obtain every available advantage under the tax system while avoiding the multitude of fatal pitfalls inherent in any highly complex tax law.

The success of Clarkson, Gordon's tax practice was reflected in the steady rise in the number of its tax specialists. By the 1980s, each office had its own tax group (or at least one partner who was designated the tax specialist). Tax specialists receive special training, including the CICA in-depth tax course (which the firm helped to develop and present for the first time in 1967). Moreover, many partners have gone on executive interchanges with various government departments, including Finance and National Revenue. In recent years the National Tax Group has been led by such outstanding practitioners as Mike Denega, John Playfair, John Greene and Joe Gill.

Yet to point out the vitality and unique aspects of the tax practice is not to suggest that the tax groups are stand-alone enterprises. On the contrary, they are integrated entirely into each office, and tax partners participate fully in the firm's team approach toward its clients.

One service long provided by a number of tax specialists has been advice on the tax aspects of personal tax and financial planning. Growing demand for personalized advice led to the pulling together of a number of partners with a special interest in the area and creation of a full range of tax-related financial planning services. It has become known as the GOALS program, led by Paul Gratias. Bill Crawford, another member of the team and long-time practitioner in the area confided, "The group couldn't make up its mind what to call the program, so it was named by the printer, who wanted to get on with producing a brochure." The printer clearly understood what they were about: the term "goals" perfectly describes the service objective of the program.

By the end of 1980, there were 149 tax specialists in the firm, including 48 partners. Today, there are over 240 staff members in tax groups across the country, including over 80 partners. With yet another round of income tax reform on the table and commodity tax reform on the horizon, and given the increasing revenue needs of governments, continued growth in this practice area seems assured.

III

One area that Duncan Gordon was especially interested in was the evolving relationship between Clarkson, Gordon and Woods, Gordon. The two firms were drawing closer and closer together as clients demanded a broader, more complete range of services. Increasingly, the two associated firms became more aware of what the other could offer, and it made good business sense to co-operate to the fullest. In 1970, there were still two distinct operations, with separate pools for profit-sharing. "We had mainly what we call an accounting, auditing and tax group," David Lay explained, "and then we had our consulting group, which was a separate firm in name and accountability, and even in organization." All this was about to change.

For most of the preceding decade, Woods, Gordon was directed by Geoffrey P. Clarkson, the great-grandson of Thomas Clarkson. Geoff Clarkson obtained his C.A. in 1937 and six years later, in 1943, became a partner in Clarkson, Gordon. The following year he became a member of the first Board of Directors of the new J.D. Woods & Gordon Ltd. During the war, he served in the financial section of the British Purchasing Mission in New York, for which he was awarded the M.B.E. After the war, he returned to the profession and, in 1963, became Chairman of Woods, Gordon's Executive Committee.

Geoff Clarkson was remembered by one colleague as a man whose "judgement was really exceptional". He also played a key role in the formation of the Canadian Association of Management Consultants in 1963 and acted as its first President. Later, he served as the first Canadian Director of the Association of Consulting Management Engineers. In 1977, his contributions were recognized at the North American Conference of Management Consultants in New York, when he was awarded the

Geoff P. Clarkson

Management Consulting Award of Excellence. The citation was later reprinted in *Keeping Posted*: "Over the years, many people within and outside the profession have benefited from Mr. Clarkson's dedication to the cause of excellence in management consulting and from his common sense and wise judgement in the many matters to which he devoted his attention."

During Mr. Clarkson's tenure as Chairman of the Executive Committee, Woods, Gordon strengthened existing areas of service and diversified into new ones. Financial planning and cost analysis had been central to its operations since its inception, and in the 1950s and 1960s new services were added, ranging from human resource management to economic advisory services. At the same time, management consulting partners were integrated into the offices of Clarkson, Gordon, as the accounting practice spread across the country.

On the international level, Woods, Gordon participated in the formation of the Canadian International Consultants for Airport Development Limited (CINCAD), a company set up to attract assignments for the planning and construction of airports anywhere in the world. Also in 1970, Woods, Gordon dispatched John O'Callaghan to Malaysia to participate in a team of Canadian consultants working on a regional development project.

As the 1960s came to a close, more attention was paid to the relationship between the two firms. Should their separate identities be maintained, or was it time to bring the two together, to unite the talents and energies of the two into one, stronger firm? Indeed, the two were already extensively intertwined.

In 1969, before any final decision was taken, Jack Smith was appointed as the new Chairman of Woods, Gordon. Educated as an economist, Mr. Smith worked as Special Assistant to the Director of the Pulp and Paper Division in the Department of Defence Production in 1951–2, and later served on the staff of the Royal Commission on Canada's Economic Prospects, where he met Walter Gordon, who was the commission's Chairman. On Mr. Gordon's invitation, he joined Woods, Gordon in 1957; he became a partner in 1960 and a member of the Executive Committee in 1967.

Soon after he assumed the chairmanship, a small committee was formed to look into the final integration of the two firms. By 1971, all the arrangements had been made and, as David Lay put it, "we got on the bandwagon of togetherness." From this point on, the two firms acted as one internally. "It doesn't matter whether you're a Woods, Gordon partner or a Clarkson, Gordon partner," explained Don Scott, a retired Chairman of Clarkson, Gordon. "Technically, there are two partnerships. In practice, there is in fact only one. We operate as a single firm, which we are."

Jack Smith

Some differences, however, remained. For one thing, only chartered accountants can be partners in Clarkson, Gordon: all the Clarkson, Gordon partners are also partners in Woods, Gordon, but not vice versa. In addition, the make-up of the two staffs continues to be slightly different. Clarkson, Gordon recruits students straight out of university and trains them, whereas Woods, Gordon tends to hire experienced men and women from industry. Thus, Woods, Gordon personnel tend to bring more variety of experience to the firm and are, on average, a little older. Finally, because the two names were kept for external marketing, some of the old allegiances to either Woods, Gordon or Clarkson,

Gordon have been maintained. This practice has declined over the years, and today, more often than not, one refers to the auditing and the consulting partners of the firm rather than to the different firms.

On the whole, the process of unification has been a success. David Lay explained: "It was an appropriate move that responded to market needs: it cemented the team approach to client service. There are many disciplines that are needed in the professional expertise that we bring to bear when meeting clients' needs. And certainly, our objective is to put a total team concept in front of the client. And this means we have to talk as one team and as partners in that team."

Throughout most of this period, the working relationship between Woods, Gordon and the trustee practice, The Clarkson Company Limited, was also becoming much closer. This development was largely the responsibility of one man – Jack Biddell. A close boyhood friend of Ken Lemon, Jack Biddell joined Clarkson, Gordon in 1939 and obtained his C.A. in 1943. He worked as a member of Pete Little's staff for several years and became a partner in 1951. Then, with the prompting of Walter Gordon, Mr. Biddell became involved in bankruptcy and insolvency work. Although reluctant at first, Mr. Biddell soon realized that this side of the practice offered enormous potential for personal and professional growth. He became Vice-President of the trustee practice at the request of Geoffrey Clarkson, the President, and on Mr. Clarkson's retirement he assumed the presidency.

Jack Biddell remained as President until 1982, with only a short break in 1975, when he was appointed to the federal government's Anti-Inflation Board. Duncan Gordon assessed Mr. Biddell's career with these words: "There is no question that Jack Biddell is recognized as the leading expert in trustee work in Canada. Probably Jack's greatest asset is that he has never accepted the fact that something could not be done, no matter what obstacles were placed in his way. If one solution to a problem was turned down, he immediately looked for another and nearly always found one."

Jack Biddell

During his career, Jack Biddell was involved in virtually every major insolvency case in Canada, beginning with Stanrock Uranium Mines in the late 1950s. In 1966, The Clarkson Company Limited was appointed Agent for the Receiver of the Atlantic Acceptance Corporation, at that time the largest insolvency situation in Canadian history. In that same year, Mr. Biddell worked on the bankruptcy case of the Prudential Finance Corporation and had to deal with so many investors that the meeting had to be held at the Royal Alexandra Theatre in downtown Toronto. "The Prudential case marked the only time I trod the boards at the Royal Alex," Jack Biddell recalled in *Keeping Posted*: "It was the only place in town big enough to hold a meeting of the creditors who wanted to be heard. There was a lot of personal hardship. I can still hear the people shrieking."

There were other, equally exciting situations in the 1970s. In 1972, for example, The Clarkson Company Limited was appointed Receiver for Rochdale College in Toronto. "It was a big event," Jack Biddell recalled, involving more than two years of delicate negotiations with residents and police, in an effort to evacuate the building and prevent serious disturbances. That this high-profile situation was handled successfully was a credit to Jack Biddell and the company as a whole.

On the international level, in July 1973, The Clarkson Company Limited was appointed to act in the liquidation of Investors Overseas Services (IOS). The demise of IOS, a huge international mutual fund conglomerate, made international headlines and was filled with enough intrigue, fraud and adventure to fuel a spy thriller. It was the biggest task ever taken on by the company and at one time involved forty members of the staff spread over two continents. There were many frustrations and road blocks along the way (and some aspects of the case are still unsettled), but it was stimulating work and considerably enhanced the company's international reputation.

The legacy of Jack Biddell, however, can be found not so much in any one particular assignment but rather in the way he extended the trustee work tradition begun by E.R.C. Clarkson decades earlier. "When I came into this business," Mr. Biddell later recalled, "when something got into financial difficulties and couldn't be rescued, it would go into bankruptcy and you usually just thought in terms of closing the doors and calling in an auctioneer and selling off what they had." Mr. Biddell believed that the company could do far more than that: "There seemed to be so many opportunities to do better, and so we took the initiative to try to rehabilitate these businesses, and if their shareholders or existing owners didn't have the financial capability or didn't have the managerial ability, then we frequently sold the businesses as a going concern, or sold parts of them to other companies, and kept a lot of the jobs that otherwise would have disappeared."

The Clarkson Company Limited increased its efforts to shift further away from liquidating businesses in trouble toward saving them from bankruptcy. Mr. Biddell became so well known that he could go to a client's premises only at night or in secret, because if he was spotted, there would be a loss of confidence in the business, which would make saving it even more difficult. This was the "penalty of notoriety," Mr. Biddell explained. The solution was to go in for the initial investigation on an assignment under the name Woods, Gordon – to do a management survey – not to close up shop and liquidate the assets. This way, confidence could be maintained long enough to determine whether or not a business could be salvaged.

Rebuilding businesses was probably the most satisfying part of Mr. Biddell's career with The Clarkson Company Limited. "This was the thing that we took the greatest pride in," he reflected. "I don't think we ever cost anybody any money through insisting we continue to operate or hold it together while we sold it on a going-concern basis. We saved our clients scores of millions of dollars over the years doing just that. And the nice part of it is that you didn't have to turn the employees onto the street."

The Clarkson Company Limited had been built into one of the largest receivership practices in the country, and under Jack Biddell it had been recognized as the leader in the industry. Over the years, the company has served as a broadening experience for a number of the firm's partners. Among those who served with The Clarkson Company Limited were Henry Pankratz, Steve Lowden, Bill Farlinger, David Yule and Ron McKinlay (now in charge of the Canada Deposit Insurance Corporation). Many other senior partners remained, including David Richardson, Hap Stephen and Ron Isaac. Moreover, by the mid–1970s the three enterprises – Woods, Gordon, The Clarkson Company Limited and Clarkson, Gordon – had developed a closer working relationship than ever before. The demands of doing business in a more competitive and aggressive business environment, ironically, had made it necessary to unify the firms more closely, in order to provide the diversity of services required.

IV

November 10, 1973 was like most Saturdays in downtown Toronto: while the shopping areas along Bloor and Yonge Streets were bustling with crowds, the business district near King and Bay was fairly quiet. Most of the Clarkson, Gordon partners and staff members were home with their families and friends. It was just another Saturday until 9:55 p.m., when smoke-detecting equipment set off an alarm on the consoles of the security desk in the Royal Trust Tower. A call was sent to the foreman engineer on duty, who was on the scene in seconds. His worst fears were instantly confirmed – there was a fire in the south-central area of the twenty-seventh floor. The fire department was alerted and arrived barely five minutes later.

It took the fire department fifteen minutes to put the fire out; it took months for the Toronto office to recover completely from the damage. The fire started in the mail room on the twenty-seventh floor and was extinguished before it had spread very far into adjacent rooms. The mail room was gutted, and the file room and tax C.A. office nearby both suffered extensive smoke and water damage. The area was off limits for seventy-two hours, and when personnel were finally admitted, one observer described in *Keeping Posted* what they discovered: "Toppled mail carts with rubber wheels melted away by the heat and rusted lockers, their doors welded shut, were a few of the discernible signs of former office life in that area. The rest was a jumbled mass of charred paper, partitioning and furniture, topped with a tangle of wires which swung crazily from the ceiling."

Although the fire was easily contained, smoke spread throughout the building. The twenty-eighth and, to a lesser degree, the twenty-ninth floors were especially hard hit. Everything – the furniture, carpets, curtains, books and files – was covered in a layer of soot. Worse, the intense heat of the fire burst a water

114

The Canadian Armed Forces high altitude test chamber in Toronto
was used to quick-dry water-soaked, irreplaceable audit files damaged
in the fire. Stacked dripping wet inside the chamber, the papers
were taken to a simulated height of 50,000 feet, where in the
rarefied air water becomes water vapour.

pipe on the twenty-seventh floor and produced a flood on the floor
below. Only fast work by the fire department – placing tarpaulins
over filing cabinets and library stacks – prevented a major disaster.

The cause of the fire could not be determined immediately, but
arson was suspected, and the Fire Marshall's Office was called in to
investigate. Don Scott, who was at that time the Office Managing

Partner in the Toronto office and Chairman of the Management Committee, arrived close to midnight. With the permission of the fire officials, he made a preliminary survey of the damage before the area was sealed off. There was nothing else that could be done that night; he would return, along with most of the staff, early the next day to begin the long, arduous task of cleaning up and assessing the damage.

The whole firm was thankful that no one had been hurt by the fire, but there was considerable concern over the extent of damage to the file room. In this room were stored working paper files: some from 1971 and all of 1972s and 1973s. Files from before 1971 were stored either in the basement or at outside storage facilities. Fortunately, the room was not gutted, but water and smoke had ruined some files while the heat had melted the plastic containers that held them. It could have been much worse; one estimate put the damage at less than 20 percent of the files, and many of these still could be saved.

The massive clean-up operation began the next day, Sunday, November 11. Large vacuum pumps were set to work clearing the two inches of water from the floor and out of the carpets, soot was wiped off, tables and desks were washed. An emergency file room, complete with metal shelves, was set up in the cafeteria on the twenty-ninth floor. Plans were drawn up for the temporary reorganization of the offices, so that business could begin again on Monday morning.

Most members of the staff pitched in and cleaned their own desks and equipment. When access was regained to the restricted areas on the twenty-seventh floor, the "bucket brigade" went into action. As reported in *Keeping Posted*: "Partners and typists in pink and green rubber gloves, armed with cleaning rags, scrubbed away the soot and grime from furniture, books and files. The staircase in the lobby was like a department store during the Christmas rush. Staff in rubber boots, carrying buckets and detergents, passed each other, going up and down the stairs, filling and refilling plastic buckets."

Everyone let out a collective sigh of relief when it was learned that the print collection came through the ordeal with only minimal damage. Two prints that were hanging close to where the fire broke out were damaged beyond repair, but the rest were preserved. Still, over two hundred prints on the twenty-seventh floor were affected by the smoke. Eventually they were all removed and sent out for rematting, cleaning and framing.

The damaged files proved to be a more intractable problem, but an ingenious solution was found. On some, it was possible merely to snip away the curled and brown edges and use the files as they were; on others a chemical process was used to bring out the type. The largest problem, however, was water damage – it would take months for the stacks of files to dry out completely, and even then they would be permanently damaged by mildew. An innovative short-cut was found, thanks to the hard work of Jim Bunton, the Assistant Office Managing Partner in Toronto, and the good graces of a client – Spar Aerospace. Mr. Bunton investigated the process in which wet papers are dried in a vacuum chamber. As the air is removed from the chamber, the water is sucked from the paper and absorbed into the thinning atmosphere. Spar Aerospace put Mr. Bunton in touch with the Armed Forces Base at Downsview, where a chamber of sufficient size could be found. Permission was granted by the Armed Forces, and thus began "Operation Paper Dry." Forty wire baskets of wet files were placed in the chamber and were taken to a simulated altitude of fifty thousand feet. The whole affair lasted almost a week, but in the end it was proclaimed a complete success.

Thanks to the hard work and unselfish determination of the staff, the firm was back on its feet in days. In fact, business resumed immediately and continued unfalteringly throughout the clean-up. Some of the damage, particularly on the southeast side of the twenty-sixth floor, could not be repaired immediately and would have to wait for major renovations in the new year. And there would always be reminders; one staffer commented in *Keeping Posted*: "There will now be easy chronological identification [of the files] by colour. They'll be known as BF files and AF files – before the fire and after the fire."

V

Throughout the long period of change through which the firm passed during these years, one thing remained constant: all partners were expected to give something back to the community and to the profession. "There was a feeling among the partners," Alex Adamson later explained, "that they must be generous in their contributions and they must get involved in some organization." There were no written rules dictating this kind of activity, Mr. Adamson continued: "It was done by example. The senior partners were always active in community affairs; we just assumed that you should be."

The benefits of community and professional involvement are numerous. Participation on government boards and commissions and in organizations like the Canadian Tax Foundation, the CICA and its provincial counterparts, and local boards of trade provides an opportunity for Clarkson Gordon people to become known within the profession and to have a real impact on the environment within which they work. The same can be said for contributing to charitable and community causes. Here, the firm's partners and staff play a prominent and effective role in determining the kind of community within which they live and raise their families. And participation in community affairs promotes the personal growth of the individual and, ultimately, enhances the reputation of the firm.

It would be needlessly self-serving to record a litany of community involvements of the partners of the firm. Suffice it to say that behind the name of virtually every partner there would be a list of charitable and community causes in which he or she was involved, ranging from the United Way to the Canadian Arthritis Society, from UNICEF to the Red Cross, from hospitals to university advisory boards, and from local community schools and churches to large cultural institutions.

In 1973, several members of the firm launched an especially ambitious project – the Clarkson Gordon Foundation. The Foundation was established as a tribute to Jack Wilson on his retirement in 1973. Its objective was "to promote interest in and the study of accountancy in all its branches and related disciplines." This goal could be achieved in a number of ways: for example, through the establishment or support for endowments, scholarships and fellowships for students in accountancy or some related discipline, or through the support for the research and writing of articles and books on accounting.

The Foundation's first project gives an indication of the different ways in which the study of accounting could be enhanced. In May 1975, a financial accounting workshop was sponsored by the Foundation in an effort to bring together practising accountants and academics to exchange ideas. The three-day workshop was held at Toronto's York University and examined several papers on accounting topics, including one by Ross Skinner. From these beginnings, the Clarkson Gordon Foundation has continued to stimulate research in and support of the study of accounting in Canada.

For Jack Wilson, retirement from the firm meant the beginning of a whole new career. In 1973, he became Chairman of the federal Independent Committee for the Review of the Office of the Auditor General of Canada, a job on which he worked for the next seventeen months. In April 1975, the Wilson Report was tabled in the House of Commons, at which time Mr. Wilson accepted a post as a member of the Ontario Securities Commission. Mr. Wilson did not see all the effects of his work, for he died suddenly on July 16, 1976. But many recommendations of the Wilson Report were put into effect. As one citation to Mr. Wilson noted, it "has proven to be the single most important influence on the Office of the Auditor General in the first 100 years of its history."

In the area of research, Ross Skinner and Rod Anderson continued on the ground-breaking course they established in the 1960s, with the publication of several more books on auditing and accounting. In 1972, Mr. Skinner published *Accounting Principles: A Canadian Viewpoint*, a Canadian look at the field. Thereafter he continued to research and write about accounting; he was awarded an honorary doctorate from Brock University in 1979 and the

Award of Outstanding Merit from the Institute of Chartered Accountants of Ontario in 1984. He retired from the firm in 1983, but not from research; in 1987, he published *Accounting Standards in Evolution*, perhaps his finest work.

Rod Anderson, meanwhile, after developing the firm's training program for computer auditing with Ron Gage, went on to investigate statistical sampling. Together with Don Leslie, who studied for his C.A. with the firm in the 1960s and rejoined it in 1971, Mr. Anderson developed a new auditing technique called dollar-unit sampling. Rather than using individual invoices or receivable balances as the basic sampling unit, the new technique used "dollar units," i.e., picking, say, every 50,000th dollar rather than selecting every 100th invoice. Dollar-unit sampling gives greater stress to larger invoices and limits the margin of error by reducing the chances of overlooking a mistake in a large account, the proverbial "needle in a haystack". As Messrs. Anderson and Leslie and Professor A.D. Teitlebaum of McGill University explained in a 1973 article in the *Canadian Chartered Accountant*, "Dollar-unit sampling solves the haystack needle problem in a rather ingenious way – by conceptually chopping up the large needle into a lot of little needles, which then occur with a sufficient frequency that they have a chance of being detected by the sample. Large errors clustered in large accounts are almost impossible to detect by unstratified physical-unit sampling but are easily detected by dollar-unit sampling."

The work of Rod Anderson, Don Leslie and Professor A.D. Teitlebaum was published in book form as *Dollar-Unit Sampling, A Practical Guide for Auditors*. Today, Mr. Leslie points out, "statistical sampling is pretty widespread among auditing firms, and dollar-unit sampling, by one name or another, is more widely used than any other form of sampling." In 1980, the three authors were awarded the Wildman Medal by the American Accounting Association for the significant contribution to public accounting made by *Dollar-Unit Sampling*. The award money was donated by Messrs. Anderson and Leslie to the fledgling periodical *Auditing: A Journal of Practice and Theory*, in an effort to get it on its feet.

Efforts such as this in research and publication have maintained the firm in the vanguard of the academic side of accounting. Indeed, as Ross Skinner pointed out, only a few firms consider it important to maintain a research program at all. To him it was an indication of Clarkson Gordon's broad-mindedness that it not only permitted research but actively encouraged it. "Our firm has done more pure research than any other," Mr. Skinner was quoted in *Keeping Posted*, "and that's put us on the leading edge of accounting." Few other firms can make that claim.

VI

By the end of the 1970s, the changing business environment in Canada produced a demand for broader and more specialized services from the accounting profession and led to an increase in the number and size of mergers. "Never in history has there been such a scramble in the accounting profession to merge firms, to set up new affiliations or to undo old ones," Don Scott told one partners' conference. "Hardly a month goes by without reading in the paper of some new merger or new arrangement."

Duncan Gordon was particularly aware of the changes in the profession and business environment and, in response, he spear-headed a review of the firm's internal structure and its policies at the Partners' Conference in September 1978. The relationship with Woods, Gordon was further formalized, the committee structure was reviewed, and the roles of the various committee chairmen were redefined. All areas of the firm's operations came under close scrutiny, and most were found to be in sound working order. There was a sense that the firm's "managerial function" could be made more efficient, but only to the extent that it would enhance the "professional function". As Mr. Gordon explained to the partners, the management of the firm "should be carried out in such a way so as to enable the partners to achieve their maximum potential with a minimum of interruption or interference."

The following year, the Executive Committee announced that beginning in 1980, Clarkson, Gordon & Co. and Woods, Gordon & Co. would adopt new names by dropping the commas and the "& Co." The change to Clarkson Gordon and Woods Gordon gave

Clarkson Gordon
Woods Gordon

MEMBERS OF ARTHUR YOUNG INTERNATIONAL

Firm Name 1980

a more streamlined and standardized look to the names; it symbolized the commitment to bilingualism and reflected the trend toward togetherness that dominated the decade. "The firm is national in scope," Mr. Gordon told the partners in 1978. "It consists of several hundred individual practices carried on in many offices. Such practices are bound together by mutual interest and common loyalties, and are interdependent." These facts were not new to the partners assembled that day; indeed, the firm was founded on the principles of common loyalty and interdependence. But as the firm approached the 1980s these qualities seemed more valuable than ever before.

CHAPTER ELEVEN

The Eighties
and Beyond

"WE HAVE BEEN VERY FORTUNATE, over the years, to have had a very happy, harmonious and collegial partnership," Don Scott told the partners in 1983. "This has been, is and will be one of our greatest strengths." And the special quality that was apparent in the past was still recognizable, if somewhat difficult to define: "I believe our firm has a particular style or ethos which is hard to articulate, but which is recognized by our partners and staff and by the business community. We do not seek to produce a typical Clarkson Gordon or Woods Gordon man or woman. Such an idea is anathema to us. We applaud the individual differences in background, personality and interests of our partners and staff." But there was a "common thread" sought by the firm, Mr. Scott continued, "that of high intelligence and competence, a dedication to excellence, fierce independence and client service. Our clients are entitled to quality service which is innovative and business oriented, which is delivered in a prompt, timely fashion by independent, fearless and competent people."

Don Scott became Chairman of the Executive Committee on February 1, 1979, taking over on the retirement of Duncan Gordon. Mr. Scott began his career with Clarkson, Gordon in 1949. While still a student, he was a member of the Toronto Argonauts for three years and played in the famous "Mud Bowl Classic" Grey Cup game in 1950.

One Monday morning, Don Scott was summoned to Colonel Gordon's office. The Colonel "was sitting with his head down looking at something," Mr. Scott recalled; "I stood at attention opposite him."

"Oh, Scott," said the Colonel after a few moments, " I just wanted to tell you that I went to that football game on Saturday – first game I've been to in years – and I want to tell you that when I saw you catch that pass and go across the goal line, I was never prouder of the firm."

That was the end of the conversation, but it also was the beginning of a long and close association between the two men. Years later, Mr. Scott was given an envelope full of newspaper clippings and pictures from his football-playing days – clippings cut out and saved by the Colonel.

Don Scott received his C.A. in 1952 and became an audit partner in 1956. From 1963 to 1967 he served as the Office Managing Partner in the Montreal office, returning to Toronto in 1967. In 1972, he was elected Chairman of the Management Committee and, in 1979, became Chairman of the firm.

As Senior Partner, it fell to Mr. Scott to lead the firm into the 1980s. He brought his own philosophy and style of leadership, and left his personal stamp on most of the tough decisions taken over the next eight years. Don Scott was born with natural ability, but he earned his success through hard work and dedication to the profession. He believed that "the principal objective of the firm is to carry out its role with the highest possible competence and absolute independence, to carry it out aggressively and successfully, and to maintain the highest possible reputation with our clients, our colleagues and the public."

Don Scott shared many basic principles with his predecessors – Duncan Gordon, Jack Wilson and Walter Gordon – and he was determined to maintain the standards established by those men. "We will continue to participate fully and provide leadership in the development of our profession in Canada," Mr. Scott was quoted in *Keeping Posted* in 1979. "We will continue to seek people of intelligence, high principles and energy. And we will continue to give them responsibility, provide them with an environment where they can work, earn a good income and achieve the fullest potential." "We are the best," he added, "no doubt about it."

Don Scott

The firm Mr. Scott inherited was very large indeed. In 1979, there were 2,382 staff, including 249 partners and 366 managers. Good people had always been at the root of Clarkson Gordon's success and, as the firm expanded, it remained just as important but increasingly difficult to maintain and develop human resources to the fullest. The challenge of the next decade, then, was to maintain and, if possible, improve the level of quality and motivation of personnel and to create an environment that would foster personal and professional growth.

There were other challenges as well. In 1981, the world fell into the most severe international recession since the 1930s, and many of the firm's clients experienced very difficult times. For some, it was a triumph just to stay afloat. The recession had a strong impact on the firm (and the profession as well), especially in 1982–3, but continuing right through until 1985. The contraction of business reduced the pool of potential clients for the competing accounting firms, and existing clients increasingly demanded more cost-effective services.

The firm responded by making itself more efficient in the services it offered. "Economic conditions remain unsatisfactory in many sectors," Mr. Scott reported in his year-end message for 1983; "many of our clients continue to experience severe financial and operating difficulties, and some have not survived. Our emphasis is still focused on cost-effective audits to keep fees to a minimum and on the provision of advice and assistance in the areas of cost reduction and productivity."

One positive move by the firm was to intensify and co-ordinate its approach to industry specialization. Health care, for example, was a particular target area in which the firm had had considerable success. In that field, teams of dynamic auditing and consulting specialists began to work together on a full-range package of services, including financial planning and operations management. Bringing specialists from different backgrounds and with different strengths into a single team began to pay dividends. In one six-month period in 1983 alone, the firm was appointed auditor for three Canadian hospitals – in London, Calgary and North York. Alan Backley, who left his post as Ontario's Deputy Minister of Health to join the firm, today leads the Health Care Practice.

Another prominent area of specialization was banking. This group was led for many years by Michael Mackenzie. Mr. Mackenzie was recognized as the leading auditor of banks and on his retirement from the firm was asked to become Canada's first Superintendent of Financial Institutions. His mandate covers not only banks, but other federally regulated financial institutions, including insurance and trust companies.

In 1982, a specialization group for high-technology industry was formed, comprising partners from across the country who had special interest and expertise in the new technologies. The group met regularly to exchange ideas and information and to discuss recent trends in the business community. Each group member, in turn, met with people in other associations and committees in the field with a view to establishing a national network of contacts. The group continues its leadership role in this key area under the direction of Peter Farwell.

At present, there are twenty-four industry specialization areas, of which the key ones are: financial services, real estate, health care, high-tech, manufacturing, natural resources and retailing.

The whole firm, meanwhile, embraced micro-computer technology. By 1985, it had over 500 micro-computers in use in all segments of the practice. A number of custom-designed micro-based audit tools were developed, and nearly every audit partner, manager and staff member had received in-house training. Some of the firm's micro-software was used by other Arthur Young International firms. By the end of 1985, Mo Hewitt, the firm's National Director of Information Technology, could state proudly in *Keeping Posted*: "All of our auditors can now be truly called computer auditors. They have the training and the tools to use micro-computers in the audit of the computerized accounts of our clients. We have also become an important micro-software development centre within AYI."

In other areas, too, the firm continued to make progress in an otherwise difficult time. The Mergers and Acquisitions (M&A) Group, which traces its roots back to the formation of the Business Valuation Group in 1972, expanded and broadened its focus in the 1970s and early 1980s through its work on projects for the Newfoundland, Manitoba and Saskatchewan governments. Moreover, with the restructuring of many industries during the recession (as businesses shed some of their less successful components), new opportunities arose for the Group. Under Fraser Mason, the M&A practice grew rapidly and became an even larger asset to the accounting and auditing practice. More recently, the Group has participated in a divestiture project for Eaton's Financial Services and, in 1986, gave financial advice and took on a major role with respect to the acquisition of Canadair for Bombardier. Today, the M&A Group consists of more than thirty men and women in Toronto and other offices, including Calgary, Vancouver and Montreal.

Another significant development was the Entrepreneurial Services Group. Originally formed in 1978 in Toronto, the Small Business Group, led by Walter Stothers (now Ontario's Agent General in New York), evolved into the Toronto Business Advisory Group (better known as T-BAG) in an effort to attract entrepreneurial clients in the Toronto area. Its primary focus was on business advice rather than on auditing. The goal, one partner explained, "was to play the role of the VP Finance of medium- to smaller-size companies."

The success of T-BAG was immediate and rapid: it increased from 23 people in 1979 to 45 a year later, and was attracting nearly five new clients a week. More recently, the name has been changed to the Entrepreneurial Services Group (ESG) and in 1986, when the staff and partners numbered 120, one large section was split away under the direction of Garry West, to open the York Region Office. Many of the clients that benefited from the help of the ESG have remained with the firm and, today, several other offices have created their own Entrepreneurial Services Groups.

The intensity of the recession kept activity for The Clarkson Company Limited, (now Clarkson Gordon Inc.) at a high level. The diversification, specialization and efficiency measures taken by the firm, meanwhile, began to have some impact, as the worst effects of the recession subsided. "Despite the troubled waters through which we sail," Don Scott wrote, "the firm continues to make good progress. Our industry specialization groups are gaining increased recognition and are attracting new clients. New products and services are being introduced, not only in the specialist areas but in the audit area as well. The development of computerized audit planning and procedures, as well as of techniques such as regression analysis, are proceeding at a rapid pace."

The unfortunate business climate of the early 1980s accelerated existing trends in business and forced Canadian accounting firms to become much more aggressive and openly competitive in their efforts to attract new clients. Competition from other major accounting firms intensified and a new challenge appeared from Certified General Accountants (and, to a lesser degree, from Certified Management Accountants), who have become much more determined in their search for a place in the public accounting field.

Many partners would agree that these developments were a turn for the worse. In the past, Don Scott recalled, "it was a gentlemanly profession in many ways; there wasn't price-fixing or deals or any of those sorts of things going on among the various firms, but they all treated one another with a courtesy and respect, you know, a real professional attitude. We didn't advertise." In addition, "you expected that the way you grew and prospered was by word-of-mouth reputation; if you did fine work and you did it at an appropriate price, people would come to you. You built your reputation and you rode along with it." Today, it is not uncommon for clients to change auditors, even if they are satisfied with the service provided. Moreover, the various firms may compete for audits and advertise their services within the business community.

With the recession in the early 1980s, the firm, under the guidance of Don Scott, Bill Farlinger and Steve Lowden, started to focus on the marketing side of the profession and this transition was not always an easy one. Bill Farlinger explained: "Twenty-five years ago good work brought its own reward. Customers came to us. Existing customers stayed with us because we did good work. Business life is much more competitive and complicated than that nowadays. You still have to do good work, but you have to be able to sell yourself, you have to sell the work, and you have to go out and get it within the professional responsibilities that we have. We've reacted well to that, but it has been hard work. It's modified the mentality of the firm by adding a marketing mode to the long-standing dimension of providing quality client service. I think that's one of the most significant changes that's happened in the last twenty-five years."

The kinds of people in the firm are changing too. New staff

members are every bit as talented and dedicated as staffers were a generation ago; indeed, most come to the firm already versed in computer language and other business skills. Yet the rise of the two-income family has increased the flexibility of young C.A.s at the outset of their careers and has made it more difficult for the firm to move people from one office to another. At the same time, there are many attractive opportunities in the business world, and new professionals (as well as existing managers and partners) are more inclined to change jobs over the course of their careers.

In an effort to attract the brightest people possible, each office has a recruiting team, which is given responsibility for the local university. By making a contribution to the university in a variety of ways, such as lecturing and participating in alumni affairs, each recruiting team helps to maintain the firm's high profile on campus.

Each year, approximately three hundred new accounting staff members are hired and given on-the-job training as they study and prepare for the Uniform Final Examinations. Clarkson Gordon staff accountants are introduced to the firm's unique staff structure which consists of a partner, two managers and four or five staff members under each manager. In contrast to the "pooling" system in other large firms, Clarkson Gordon encourages more direct responsibility, while making it easier to identify strengths and monitor areas in need of improvement in new members. The staff system also produces closer relationships between staff and partners, which assists morale, development and evaluation and often leads to life-long friendships. Moreover, this staff structure provides consistency and continuity to clients – two important factors sometimes missing in a pooling system.

The Clarkson Gordon staff structure also lends itself to the increasingly important areas of quality control and staff evaluation. The more demanding and competitive business environment and the growing size of the firm have led to the introduction of more formal staff and partner evaluations. The greatest challenge in the area of personnel is to motivate and retain the best of the new staff – to keep them challenged and help them stay in the field.

The task is larger than turning them into C.A.s; the real goal is to turn them into businesspeople.

The same high standards apply to Clarkson Gordon's administrative staff, which comprises a significant portion of the total personnel. Indeed, the administrative staff provides the essential support needed to make the firm operate smoothly and efficiently. Over the years the Administrative Services Groups in the various offices have demonstrated strong leadership.

By far the greatest change in personnel has been in the number of women who have joined the firm. Beginning in the 1960s, more and more women have turned their attention to the accounting profession and have entered business schools and universities. In the 1970s, many female graduates were being taken on as new staff accountants, starting the long climb up the ladder. In 1978, there were 16 female managers and 250 female staff members in the firm; the first woman partner was appointed in 1980. From 1977 to 1985, women represented 35 percent of the annual intake; by 1986 the ratio had jumped to the 40–44 percent range. Today, Clarkson Gordon has 19 female partners, 187 female managers and 605 women on the professional staff. Now, many women have assumed positions of leadership in the firm and the profession; Heather Shannon of the Vancouver office, for example, became the first female President of the Institute of Chartered Accountants of British Columbia in 1987. But the rise in the number of women in the firm has not really been the result of a conscious policy, Mr. Scott points out: "Our approach to recruiting has been fairly simple and straightforward. We've just said to our recruiters: 'You get the best people you can find.'"

The people in Woods Gordon were confronted with the same challenges and concerns that faced the accounting practice. In the 1980s, Woods Gordon was not only the oldest full-service management consulting firm in the country, it was also the largest. The record of the firm over the previous decade was impeccable in terms of growth and client service, and the joint practice with Clarkson Gordon was prospering.

In 1981, Jack Smith retired from the chairmanship of Woods

Gordon to take up a government position working on the National Energy Program, and he was succeeded by John Wilson. A graduate of the University of Toronto, Mr. Wilson worked in private industry before joining Woods, Gordon in 1963. He became a partner in 1967 and specialized in general management and marketing problems. He also served as the founding Chairman of the Canadian Institute for Advanced Research. John Wilson was succeeded in the Chairmanship of Woods Gordon in 1985 by Leonard Delicaet. Mr. Delicaet joined Woods, Gordon in 1960, following work in the pulp and paper industry and graduation from McGill University and the Carnegie-Mellon Graduate School of Industrial Administration.

The close association of Woods Gordon and Clarkson Gordon developed from the growing interdependence of the accounting and consulting partners, as the one side made use of the services provided by the other. Areas such as Mergers and Acquisitions and Value-for-Money Auditing, Mr. Wilson wrote, "which were developed and introduced initially by partners in accounting and consulting respectively, have now moved to positions which can best be described as between the two practices."

An example of the various disciplines working together on one project was the major review of the operations of Revenue Canada carried out in 1985. It was led by Bill Farlinger with John Playfair (tax), Alan Backley (consulting), Glen Cronkwright and David Leslie (both tax), Tony Grant (consulting), Cheryl Campbell Steer (consulting) and many other personnel from both Woods Gordon and Clarkson Gordon.

The recently acquired project to track mail delivery for the Canada Post Corporation will put to good use the many special talents of dozens of consulting and auditing professionals. "The objective of the project," explains Len Delicaet, "is, first, to develop a methodology by which you can measure the performance of the Post Office delivery system against predetermined standards and, secondly, to then fabricate mail, put it in the system and measure when it is received by a panel of 2,500 recipients in every province in Canada."

The idea of tracking mail is relatively straightforward, but its implementation is extremely complex. "After a six-month research and design process," *Keeping Posted* reported, "the firm has now set up and is operating its own mail-manufacturing plant to produce test mail, a telephone centre to take calls, and a computer centre to generate the mail-making instructions and produce the performance reports." Total anonymity is essential, and the mail has to be produced in all shapes and sizes and randomly distributed across the country. When one of the pieces of mail is received by one of 2,500 individuals and businesses, it is reported to the firm's telephone and computer centre. The project is enormous by any standards, involving over 60,000 pieces of mail randomly distributed to more than sixty centres across the country.

In 1988, Mr. Delicaet assumed leadership of the firm's Industry Specialization Program and became Chairman of the Information Management Committee. He was succeeded as Chairman of Woods Gordon by Henry Pankratz, who joined the firm in 1961 and became a partner in 1968. Mr. Pankratz left his position as Office Managing Partner in the Vancouver office to take over as Chairman.

II

Everyone who is taken on by the firm becomes a member of the Clarkson Gordon "family". The sense of collegiality is encouraged among present staff and is preserved among the expanding alumni. Regular contact with alumni is maintained through the firm's directory and newsletter. Many members of the staff establish close friendships during their years with the firm, and the alumni network provides the opportunity to keep in touch with those who have left. In addition, because many of those who leave go to existing clients, participation in alumni affairs helps to strengthen the bonds between client and firm.

Clarkson Gordon takes great pride in the fact that many of its alumni go on to make important contributions in business, industry, government and the arts and sciences. Indeed, there are hundreds of men and women who have served with the firm at some point in their careers – as partners, managers, staff accountants or administrative staff – who have gone on to pursue other interests. Each has contributed to the firm in his or her own way, while few have left without taking with them some of the values, pride and tradition of Clarkson Gordon.

The pride that the firm takes in its alumni is evidenced through the Clarkson Gordon *Alumni Directory*, which runs to almost 300 pages. "Whether you are a Clarkson Gordon/Woods Gordon alumnus of one or fifty years," Mr. Farlinger explained in an open letter to the alumni, "I am sure that all of you feel, as I do, that this firm is a special place. And we are proud of the company we keep in both senses of the word – the firm itself, and the friends and colleagues with whom we have worked." A casual glance through the firm's Directory or a recent edition of *Who's Who* reveals the hundreds of Clarkson Gordon men and women who have made their mark in the community. Today, this list includes the leaders of some of the largest corporations in the country as well as senior individuals in government and in the universities – indeed, in virtually every field of human endeavour.

The CICA recognizes "outstanding service to the accounting profession" by bestowing on certain individuals the Certificate of Merit. Only fourteen members of the Canadian profession have received such an honour and five of them are partners or alumni of the firm. In 1988, Marcel Caron and Marcel Bélanger received the Certificate of Merit. Duncan Gordon received it in 1987, Ross Skinner in 1985 and Gertrude Mulcahy in 1982.

III

The development of industry specialization and the rise of computer technology in the 1980s was strongly felt in the offices of Clarkson Gordon across the country. In Ottawa, for example, the firm's audit and consulting groups focused on servicing the growing number of high-tech clients in the Ottawa valley (or "Silicon Valley North," as some people call it). Today there are over 100 men and women working in the office, making it one of the larger offices of the firm.

In Atlantic Canada, an office was opened in St. John's, Newfoundland, in 1973, when the firm merged with Read, Watson, Hyslop and Cooper, an established practice that traced its origins back to 1906. Clarkson Gordon had long wanted a "beachhead" in Newfoundland, and the union gave Clarkson Gordon an immediate and valuable presence in Newfoundland's capital.

Ten years later, in 1983, the Newfoundland office merged with Warr, Saunders, Blackwood and Hoskins, which brought in three more partners and twelve staff members, making Clarkson Gordon one of the largest firms in St. John's. Four of the St. John's partners have, over this period, served as presidents of the Newfoundland Institute of Chartered Accountants: Don Blackwood, Jim Cavanagh, Steve Gallagher and Don Warr. Today, under the leadership of Bob Healey, Clarkson Gordon is the largest professional accounting firm in St. John's.

The Toronto region also went through a period of unprecedented expansion in the late 1970s and early 1980s. In response to the tremendous growth and the increasing pressure on the downtown office, suburban or regional offices were established in Mississauga (1976) to the west and in Scarborough (1977) to the east. The Office Managing Partners in these two offices are now Dave Stephen and Ron Buckle, respectively. In 1986, as we have seen, the York Region office opened for business to the north of Toronto, with Garry West as Managing Partner. The Mississauga office continues to grow as the city flourishes. Plans are that by 1989, the office will have doubled in size in terms of personnel and will move into the Clarkson Gordon tower of a new commercial development in the heart of the Mississauga business district.

In 1983, Clarkson Gordon merged with Needham, Underhill & Partners in Barrie, which gave the firm a solid base in a growing area. All the regional offices are well situated to service clients moving out of the downtown area to new suburban locations.

The office in downtown Toronto is the largest of any C.A. firm in

Canada, with 170 partners and 1,200 staff members, and is substantially larger than most C.P.A. offices in the United States. Jim Bunton is the Office Managing Partner (and also an Executive Partner), responsible for the Toronto audit, tax, insolvency and mergers and acquisitions practices. Because of its enormous size and the wide scope of its business, the firm has restructured the Toronto office's operations. For example, in an effort to give the audit and tax practices greater focus, these practices were divided into five groups of about fifteen partners each who concentrate on specific areas of interest, in addition to their normal practices. Each of these groups on its own would be larger than most of the firm's practice offices. The areas of some of the groups (and the current practice directors) are: international clients and activities (Colin Lipson), the retailing sector (Owen Menzel), mining, manufacturing and real estate (Grant Jones), financial services (Mark O'Regan) and entrepreneurial services and high tech (Peter Farwell). Eric Ostfield co-ordinates the overall delivery of tax services to Toronto clients.

The Toronto office is bursting at the seams. In 1982, three floors in the National Bank Building, a few blocks away from the Toronto-Dominion Centre, were rented to accommodate the overflow. By 1987, however, it was clear that the firm was outgrowing its existing space in the Royal Trust Tower, and, with the firm's lease coming to an end, a committee was brought together to research all the available downtown offices to find a suitable new location.

From a variety of possible sites the number was narrowed down to two, with a site near the southeast corner of Yonge and Adelaide Streets as the inside favourite. This location held many attractions, but some members of the committee had reservations about moving to the perimeter of Toronto's financial district. Although only a few blocks east of the T-D Centre, this locale might isolate the firm by cutting down on personal contact between the staff and other business people. Such contact is essential for maintaining

Opposite: The Clarkson Gordon Tower, 1991

137

close business relationships. Besides, Clarkson Gordon had always been at the very centre of Toronto's financial district, and it seemed illogical to change that now.

Before any final arrangements were made, the firm was approached by The Toronto-Dominion Bank and Cadillac Fairview Corporation with a proposal that was too exciting to turn down. Approval had been received from the City to construct a fifth tower in the T-D Centre, and the Centre's management proposed that the new building be named the Clarkson Gordon Tower, with the firm as its principal occupant. The firm could not resist such a remarkable offer. As John Playfair, Chairman of the search committee explained, "the fact that we will be the only accounting firm in the country to have a tower named after us in a main banking complex will substantially underline the prestige and significance of the firm in the Toronto financial community." Indeed, the new building will provide a landmark home that over time will come to mean to present and future partners and staff what 15 Wellington Street did in the past.

The new thirty-storey Clarkson Gordon Tower is slated for occupancy in early 1991. The firm will hold a long-term lease and will occupy the top fifteen stories with provision to expand as needed. Housing both the Toronto office and the firm's National Departments, the tower will sit astride the historic site of the old Toronto Stock Exchange Building. It will resemble the four other towers in the T-D Centre, but it will also preserve the façade of the original building (and its marvellous frieze, *Procession of Industry* by Canadian artist Charles Comfort). The project will be an impeccable blend of old and new — mixing state-of-the-art style and technology with the elegance and charm of historic Toronto. "The new offices will reflect the tradition, history and style of Clarkson Gordon," Mr. Playfair adds, "and they will also reflect the future vision of the firm, in that they will be technologically advanced in every respect."

Another area of dynamic growth in the 1980s was Quebec. In 1981, the Quebec City office, under the direction of Raymond Lavoie, merged with Bélanger, Dallaire, Gagnon & Associés, a successful and respected local firm with an expanding base of clients. Many of these clients were expanding outside Quebec and needed the connection with a national firm and the specialized services that it could provide; Clarkson Gordon received an influx of talented people and a new major client – Bombardier. Overnight the firm became the largest in Quebec City.

Marcel Bélanger was a prominent public accountant and economist. His career included high-profile appointments as Chairman of the Quebec Royal Commission on Taxation, economic adviser to several Quebec governments and President of the CICA. At the time of the merger, the Quebec City practice was led by Charles Pelletier, a prominent chartered accountant who had been President of the Quebec Order and Chairman of the Canadian Tax Foundation. Both Charles Pelletier and Marcel Bélanger were professors at Laval University, and this led to a very valuable and close relationship with the institution. Subsequently, this thriving practice has been led by Denis Desautels and Yvon Fortin.

The success in Quebec City was repeated just outside Montreal in 1984, when the firm made a strategic decision to locate an office in Laval. This growing community was seen as an area of tremendous potential, and an effort was made to find a suitable local firm to merge with. After some investigation, it was decided that Viau, Rouleau, Brosseau & Associés offered the most potential, and on February 1, 1984, the Laval office opened its doors for business. The office experienced large growth in clientele, including the audit for Canadair (which had been acquired by Bombardier). In July 1987, the office moved to new quarters, and today, under the direction of Michel Viau, there are more than fifty people on staff, making it the second largest firm in the Laval area.

Business in Montreal was expanding to the South Shore as well, and in 1988 the firm merged with Adam, Authier, Boyer et Associés, the majority of whose clients are small businesses. The present Office Managing Partner is Serge Boyer.

The Quebec offices have been very successful in capitalizing on the new business climate in the province. The introduction of the Quebec Stock Savings Plan in 1979, for example, produced a surge

Charles Pelletier

of economic activity. Today the entrepreneurial spirit is riding high, and the future for business in the province is bright. In Quebec, as in the rest of the country, the offices of Clarkson Gordon are developing local clients as well as producing a whole new generation of talented and industrious young people who will one day assume responsibility for the direction of the firm.

III

Throughout the 1980s, the international dimension of Canadian business has taken on new importance, as Canadian corporations spread their operations abroad and as foreign firms continue to look to Canada as a target for investment. Such developments have special relevance for Clarkson Gordon, because as clients enter the international business arena and, for example, list their shares on the London and Tokyo exchanges, it becomes essential for the firm to be able to communicate effectively with the other member firms of Arthur Young International. Never before has the need for strong international connections been so great.

Arthur Young International was an enormous organization by the end of September 1988. The association had grown to over four hundred offices in seventy-two countries. AYI included 2,900 partners, and the total number of personnel passed the 33,000 mark. World-wide revenues for the year were U.S. $2.053 billion, representing a 20 percent gain over 1987. Any Canadian company with operations abroad can be assured of receiving first-class service virtually anywhere in the world, and foreign firms can be confident that they will receive the same high quality of service in Canada that Clarkson Gordon offers its domestic clients.

AYI's principal roles are to set standards throughout the AYI network, to oversee and control the quality of work done for clients and to refer work of an international nature to member firms. An Executive Office has been established, and a Management Council representing the members meets regularly. An important function of the Management Council is to identify mutual interests and to establish common policies for the AYI network. There are also some promotional programs to help demonstrate the common interests of AYI members. In 1981, for example, a new, stylized AYI symbol was introduced for use by all the constituent firms, and other efforts were made to cement the international relationship.

A number of international committees have been organized over the years to deal with specific areas, such as accounting and auditing, taxes, consulting and, more recently, audit automation. Further, the Executive Office and Management Council sponsor meetings of partners from all member countries so that they can exchange ideas and get to know each other personally and professionally, in an effort to ensure that clients' business needs are met. "What we are trying to do," explained David Wishart, "is to

141

get people in the same field meeting with one another in order to develop mutual trust and confidence so that each is quite happy to introduce their clients to the other."

A significant development was the decision taken in 1986 to switch to Apple Macintosh technology in Clarkson Gordon's audit automation. Apple is a long-time client, and in the United States, Arthur Young had already switched to Apple computers; it became imperative for Clarkson Gordon to use compatible software. Given the international environment, it was impossible for the firm to do all its research and development on its own. Clarkson Gordon could not be expected "to reinvent the wheel," David Lay explained, and "because we were on different tracks, in terms of the hardware and the software, we couldn't really talk to each other." Closer liaison with Arthur Young was necessary, especially in computer technology. "We simply had to share costs," Mr. Lay concluded, "we had to learn from their experiences and they from ours."

The switch to "Mac" was the precursor of further international co-operation within AYI. Clarkson Gordon, along with AYI firms in the United States, the United Kingdom and the Netherlands, is developing a common audit methodology to be used in those countries. In that connection, an international audit manual, with appropriate local country content, has been developed. Significant Canadian input has been provided by Ron Gage, Randy Billing and Don Cockburn.

Within the AYI network, Clarkson Gordon is the second largest national firm (in terms of annual revenue), behind only Arthur Young (U.S.). Many Clarkson Gordon and Woods Gordon partners have played key roles on AYI committees. Bill Farlinger serves on the Executive Committee of the Management Council, and the firm has had representatives on the four AYI advisory committees: Accounting and Auditing, Personnel Development, Tax and Management Services.

In 1986, Clarkson Gordon took a financial interest in Arthur Young Southeast Asia, an umbrella firm with interests in five countries on the Pacific Rim: Hong Kong, Indonesia, Malaysia,

Singapore and Thailand. Moreover, because of the activity of Canadian business in Barbados, Clarkson Gordon has taken an interest in the Barbados firm of Arthur Young.

The firm has a Clarkson Gordon partner, Terry Scandrett, and three managers resident in Hong Kong serving Canadian clients and assisting Hong Kong residents who are interested in Canada. Every summer, Canadian staff members go to Australia and New Zealand; and representatives from these two countries come to Canada in the winter to assist in each other's busy seasons. Clarkson Gordon has sixty former staff members working in Arthur Young offices around the world.

Like other international firms, AYI consists of a network of independent national firms from around the world. However, unlike English-speaking affiliates of other international accounting firms, Clarkson Gordon has kept its own name.

That there would be benefits from adopting the Arthur Young name is evident. "Our Canadian clients would better appreciate the fact that we were an international firm," Bill Farlinger explains, "because there is a lot of power in a name. And international clients coming into Canada would recognize us as a firm that they knew." So why keep the Clarkson Gordon name? For one thing it is a matter of pride – in the history of the firm and in its Canadian identity. For another, Clarkson Gordon already has the most widely known and respected name in the country. As Mr. Farlinger puts it: "You don't give up the best-recognized name in the country easily."

Questions such as these have to be dealt with on a regular basis by Bill Farlinger, who became Chairman of the Executive Committee and Senior Partner in February 1987. A native of Toronto and a graduate of the University of Toronto, Mr. Farlinger joined the firm in 1951. Over the course of his career, he worked in Vancouver, Toronto and Montreal and served as Office Managing Partner in the latter two. In addition, he served as President of The Clarkson Company Limited for a few years when Jack Biddell was appointed to the Anti-Inflation Board. In 1979, he became Chairman of the Operations Policy Committee.

Outside the firm, Mr. Farlinger has been President of the Royal Canadian Golf Association and Chairman of the University of Toronto's Presidents' Committee.

As Senior Partner, Bill Farlinger strove both to continue the process of change initiated by Don Scott and to introduce his own particular goals and areas that he wished to see developed. Computer services and mergers and acquisitions, for example, were considered to be two key growth areas. In addition, Mr. Farlinger wanted to continue to foster close relations with AYI and open up Clarkson Gordon in its dealings with clients to make Clarkson Gordon more competitive and responsive to the changing business environment. What was needed was a top-to-bottom review of the firm, its policies and its goals. Thus began the long and fruitful process of drawing up Clarkson Gordon's current strategic plan.

Several alternative versions of the plan were made. In 1986, the Executive Partners produced a draft strategic plan which was circulated to offices around the country. Once the offices had responded, a new draft was prepared at a two-day conference in Toronto, attended by fifty-one people: the Executive Partners, the Operations Policy Committee, all the Office Managing Partners, National Directors, Practice Directors and other senior members of the firm.

After this meeting of the "Group of 51", the revised draft of the plan was returned to the partnership as a whole. After receiving further comments and criticisms, the Group of 51 met once more to finalize the text. It was an extraordinary experience. "When we got into the process we found enormous interest at the partner level," Mr. Farlinger said. "What developed was a highly creative participation by all the partners in the development of the strategic plan."

Yet to come was implementation. Work on the plan was completed in April 1987, and the final version was presented to the partners at the annual meeting in May. All 400, in discussion groups, reviewed the plan, ranked the implementation activities, and identified the resources and personal commitment necessary to move the plan forward. Each office subsequently undertook to

William A. Farlinger

develop its own plan, which would fit under the larger umbrella of the national plan.

Staff members, as well as partners, have been involved in the discussions and implementation, whether in national conferences or in local activities. The degree of participation varies, depending on the management style of the practice unit, but the senior members of the firm encourage staff involvement. Staff members will be implementing many of the ideas, and they are doing no more than responding to one of the fundamentals of the firm's culture, applicable to both the partners and themselves: reliance on intelligent and competent individuals who are dedicated to excellence. They will be doing it in a changing and challenging atmosphere as well, where the newer staff members may require different conditions in which to motivate themselves, with shifting demands toward more meaningful work, a balanced life-style and a desire for a closer relationship between effort and reward – another management challenge for which the firm is already seeking solutions.

However rigorous the development of the national plan, however systematic the subsequent development of local plans, success would be uncertain without the certainty of enduring and intrinsic underlying values. The strategic plan outlines the values that Clarkson Gordon strives to uphold and sets out the direction in which the firm should head. But the process of implementation will be an ongoing one. "After lengthy and thorough examination," it was noted, "it is evident that there are no magic solutions – no single products or services, no unique directions or programs – to achieve and sustain a clearly dominant position in our fields. We must all work with energy, dedication and consistency towards our goals, emphasizing those areas where our execution can be improved or where a competitive advantage can be obtained."

In an effort to supplement the strategic plan and to meet better the challenges of the future, a small committee called Directions 2000 was formed in the summer of 1987 under the leadership of Henry Pankratz. The committee (described by Mr. Pankratz as a "think-tank that develops future issues that will have an impact on the firm") has a changing membership and is drawn from the practice and geographic areas of the firm. Its mandate is wide open: to consider issues and develop recommendations for the Executive Committee on how the firm should position itself to encounter opportunities or potential threats in the years ahead.

What are the challenges and goals of the next decade? How will the firm adapt to the changing business environment? What role will government play in business, and how will that affect the profession? Extrapolating from existing trends, it is clear that there will be more competition and more competitors in the future, also coming from non-traditional sources such as the banking industry. Moreover, the impact of technology on the profession has already been felt strongly, and the implications for the future are profound. Not only will automation affect the way clients do business, but it will also provide new freedoms and place new demands on the staff. The hardware is here; the key is to understand the technology and to apply it effectively.

An area of critical importance to the firm and to the profession, not only in Canada but in the United States and the United Kingdom as well, is the "audit expectation gap". It has become abundantly clear that there are serious gaps between the public's expectations of audits and what an auditor should reasonably be expected to accomplish. This gap is clearly demonstrated with the continuing examination of the failures of financial institutions in several countries. In Canada, the failure of two western banks and difficulties with trust companies and credit unions led the CICA to establish, in 1986, a Commission to Study the Public's Expectations of Audits. The Macdonald Commission reported in 1988 and dealt with a number of important issues. Many of the same issues were reported on earlier by the Treadway Commission in the United States. Both argued for stronger corporate governance and for strengthening the position of the auditors by such steps as more active involvement by audit committees.

Another area of primary significance is the growing internationalization of business. Ron Gage, Chairman of the Operations Policy Committee, explains: "Globalization of business, corporate concentrations, major international capital flows, incredibly complex financial transactions and instantaneous worldwide communications have combined to make Marshall McLuhan's global village a commercial reality. The international sophistication and depth of knowledge demanded of the professional accountant today are enormously demanding. Consequently, our Arthur Young International relationships are more important than ever before to serve effectively the international client of the late 1980s." In addition, Mr. Gage points out, "our clients, faced with intense international competition and forced to control costs in order to regain competitive positions, have put enormous pressure on audit fees. In turn, this has put severe pressure on the profession to address productivity and efficiency."

Such global factors will continue to affect Clarkson Gordon and draw it closer to the other firms that comprise AYI. This trend was acknowledged in the strategic plan: "We are fortunate in having our international relationships with the Arthur Young family. Of paramount importance to us is our relationship with the American firm. Arthur Young is clearly regarded as the top professional firm in the United States and, in the last few years, has become highly visible through a number of communications programs. This image complements that of our own firm. We have recently begun to work much more closely with Arthur Young on a number of matters, including research and business development."

Meeting the changing expectations and demands of clients will be the firm's central challenge in the next decade. It will be necessary to structure the practice in such a way as to meet those expectations and to introduce new services and expand existing ones. For example, the firm will increasingly provide more sophisticated personal and corporate tax planning for its clients. Other practice areas, such as Mergers and Acquisitions, Computer Audit and Litigation Support, will continue to expand. Moreover, attracting new clients will remain a key goal. Indeed, the firm has already made significant advances in this direction with the appointment of a National Director and the allocation of much time, effort and resources to business marketing.

National Marketing, currently led by Lonnie Tate, joined a host of National Departments developed over the last quarter-century. All of them were instituted to support the practitioner in the field across the country; each was designed to provide the kind of support that reflected the firm's commitment to excellence. The earliest departments – dealing with auditing, accounting and tax matters – had soon been joined by those devoted to personnel and educational matters. These latter two departments, currently led by Barney McGrogan and Don Johnston, have continued to provide workable solutions for the complex of people issues within

148

which the firm and profession operate. National Education Services, for example, has led in developing instructional materials and technologies: it currently delivers, with the assistance of local office instructors, some twenty thousand person-days of education annually.

Industry specialization will receive considerable attention in the years to come. The firm has already experienced great success in its industry specialization programs, and it will be increasingly important to adjust the services offered to the needs of the client. "There will be continual movement towards an industry focus," Mr. Pankratz explains. "We will have to align our services with industries as opposed to aligning them in our traditional way on a product line or service basis. So, understanding the attributes, the service needs and unique characteristics of these industries and then turning our people into specialists in those industries will be a continual challenge for many years to come."

The key to the future lies with the firm's ability to deal successfully with these and other critical issues. Still, the most important ingredient for success will be found in the individual men and women that make up the firm. And, in some respects, the future is already here. "Most of the senior partners of the future are probably already with the firm," Mr. Gage concludes. "These senior people will be a combination of those who have recently been admitted to partnership and those who are barely out of university and still working diligently on their C.A. What are their names? At this point no one knows — but they are with us!"

IV

Today, Clarkson Gordon has a staff complement in excess of thirty-three hundred and includes more than a thousand partners and managers in twenty-six offices across Canada. The list of its clients reads like a *Who's Who* of the top Canadian corporations and includes major banks, trust companies and credit unions, utilities, life and health insurance companies, broadcasting and publishing firms, universities, hospitals, municipalities, resource corporations, real estate developers, transportation and communication companies and a broad range of manufacturing and high-tech corporations. To every client – large or small – Clarkson Gordon makes a personal commitment to provide superior service.

This attention to personal service, a long-standing tradition of Clarkson Gordon, is key to maintaining and acquiring valued clients. The firm's slogan, "We take business personally," is not just a catchy phrase – each and every member of the Clarkson family lives it out every day in his or her work with clients. Each member of the firm seeks to provide superior service to clients that is intensely personal yet maintains the highest standards of competence and objectivity. This requires service that is timely and responsive, that anticipates and recognizes need and so contributes to the client's success – service that is of high quality and objectivity, which is best described as "professional excellence".

The deaths of Walter Gordon and Duncan Gordon in 1987 produced a great sense of loss among partners and staff. It also served to remind everyone of Clarkson Gordon's strong and vital links to the past. Only a few weeks before his death, Walter Gordon wrote Bill Farlinger: "I have been lucky enough to have had two very interesting jobs as well as being head of Clarkson's and Woods Gordon. But, in retrospect, I really believe I got the most kick out of being the head of the two firms." It would be difficult to find any two partners that contributed more to the firm through the course of its long history than Duncan Gordon and Walter Gordon.

Preparations for the 125th anniversary also began in 1987. An Anniversary Committee, consisting of a number of senior partners, was formed to plan the celebrations. A new logo was designed for the anniversary, and a contest was sponsored to find the best slogan. The winner was "Committed to the future, indebted to our past," which seemed to capture the spirit of the firm on the eve of its 125th birthday. "Both the past and the future are extremely important," Mr. Farlinger explained. "We have a great heritage, but it's the future that counts." After 125 years, the firm continues to benefit from the lessons of the past.

150

The past can teach us many things, but these lessons alone are not enough to guarantee success in the future. It is only the wisdom and vision of today's and tomorrow's partners that can carry Clarkson Gordon on to meet the challenges and opportunities of the next one hundred and twenty-five years.

APPENDICES

Clarkson Gordon Chronology

1864	– Thomas Clarkson was appointed Official Assignee by the Dominion government and founded the firm Thomas Clarkson & Co. in Toronto.
1870	– E.R.C. Clarkson joined his father's firm at the age of seventeen.
1872	– Thomas Clarkson retired. E.R.C. Clarkson formed the partnership Clarkson and Munro (dissolved 1877).
1874	– Thomas Clarkson died at age seventy-two.
1877	– E.R.C. Clarkson was appointed an Official Assignee and formed the firm Turner, Clarkson & Co. (dissolved 1881).
1883	– E.R.C. Clarkson commenced practice as a chartered accountant as one of the original members of the Institute of Chartered Accountants of Ontario, formed that year.
1891	– E.R.C. Clarkson and W.H. Cross formed an accounting partnership, Clarkson & Cross.
1893	– G.T. Clarkson joined his father's firm.
1898	– H.D. Lockhart Gordon entered the service of Clarkson & Cross.
1905	– H.D. Lockhart Gordon left Clarkson & Cross and started his own practice.
1907	– H.D. Lockhart Gordon and R.J. Dilworth formed the partnership Gordon & Dilworth.

1913	– The firms Clarkson & Cross and Gordon & Dilworth were dissolved. E.R.C. Clarkson, G.T. Clarkson, H.D. Lockhart Gordon and R.J. Dilworth formed the firm Clarkson, Gordon & Dilworth, with offices at 15 Wellington Street West, Toronto. (W.H. Cross retired.)
	– E.R.C. Clarkson & Sons was formed to continue the trustee practice, also at 15 Wellington Street West.
1922	– An office was opened in Montreal in the name of Clarkson, Gordon & Dilworth.
1928	– The firms Clarkson, Gordon & Dilworth, in Toronto, and McDonald, Currie & Co. (now Coopers & Lybrand), in Montreal, formed a partnership which, thereafter, carried on business in Ontario under the name Clarkson, Gordon, Dilworth, Guilfoyle & Nash and in Quebec under the name Clarkson, McDonald, Currie & Co.
1929	– Offices were opened in Windsor (closed 1934) and Ottawa (closed 1937).
1931	– E.R.C. Clarkson died at age seventy-nine.
1935	– The partnership with McDonald, Currie, & Co. was dissolved. Clarkson, Gordon, Dilworth, Guilfoyle & Nash reopened its own offices in Montreal and Ottawa. The name of the firm was changed to Clarkson, Gordon, Dilworth & Nash when H.E. Guilfoyle died.
1938	– An office was opened in Hamilton.
1939	– The firm became associated with The J. D. Woods Co. Limited, which later became Woods, Gordon & Co.
1944	– The firm Arthur Young, Clarkson, Gordon & Co. was formed to conduct business in Canada for Arthur Young & Company, and to conduct business in the United States for Clarkson, Gordon, & Co.
	– J.D. Woods and Gordon Ltd. was established.

1945	– An office was opened in Vancouver.
1946	– The name of the firm was changed to Clarkson, Gordon & Co.; E.R.C. Clarkson & Sons became the Clarkson Company partnership.
1948	– An office was opened in London, Ontario.
	– The Winnipeg practice of Black, Hanson & Co. merged with the firm, and an office opened in that city.
	– The practice of H.D. Campbell of Vancouver joined the firm.
1949	– Geoffrey T. Clarkson died.
	– The practice of Richardson & Graves of Calgary merged with the firm, and an office opened in that city.
1952	– The practice of Read, Smith & Forbes of Regina merged with the firm and an office opened in that city.
1954	– The Clarkson Company partnership was dissolved and its business was transferred to a newly formed corporation, The Clarkson Company Limited.
1955	– The practice of Charles T. Sears & Co. of London, Ontario merged with the firm.
1956	– An office was opened in Edmonton on the merger with the practice of Kinnaird, Aylen & Company.
	– W. Macintosh of Macintosh & Ross of Calgary joined the firm on dissolution of that partnership.
1957	– The practice of MacLennan & Company of Windsor, Ontario merged with the firm and an office opened in that city.
1959	– The Vancouver practice merged with that of Carter, Reid & Walden.
	– The Brazilian partnership of Arthur Young, Clarkson, Gordon & Co. established offices in Rio de Janeiro and São Paulo.
	– J.D. Woods and Gordon Ltd. was dissolved and the partnership of Woods, Gordon & Co. was formed.

1960	– The Calgary practice merged with Harvey, Morrison & Co.
	– Woods, Gordon & Co. and The Clarkson Company Limited moved from 15 Wellington Street West, Toronto to temporary quarters in the old Bank of Nova Scotia Building on Melinda Street. Clarkson, Gordon & Co. expanded into the annex structure of 15 Wellington Street West.
1962	– The firm merged with Davis, Dunn & Broughton in Kitchener and London and with Scully & Scully in Kitchener and the firm established an office in Kitchener.
	– The Quebec office opened and soon merged with DeCoster, Normandeau & Cie.
1963	– Walter Gordon retired from the firm to assume his new post as federal Minister of Finance.
1964	– The various firms that had ties with Arthur Young (U.S.) formed Arthur Young & Company (International), now known as Arthur Young International.
	– Clarkson, Gordon & Co. celebrated its 100th anniversary.
1965	– The firm merged with F.H. Black & Company of Thunder Bay, and an office opened in that city.
	– An office opened in Halifax.
	– An office opened in Ottawa.
1966	– Colonel Gordon died.
1967	– A merger with Cox & Hammett led to an office being opened in Saint John, New Brunswick.
	– Clarkson, Gordon & Co. merged with the Victoria-based firm Holt & Campion and established an office in that city.
1968	– The Regina office merged with Wicijowski, Wenaus & Company which doubled the size of the practice.
1969	– The Ottawa practice merged with Milne, Honeywell and Burpee.

1973	– A fire broke out on the twenty-seventh floor of the Royal Trust Tower and damaged files, furniture and some of the art collection.
	– An office was opened in St. John's, Newfoundland, when the firm merged with Read, Watson, Hyslop and Cooper.
1975	– The firm merged with Basin & Barsky in Regina.
1976	– The Mississauga office was established.
	– Jack Wilson died.
1977	– The Toronto Metro-East office opened.
	– The Windsor office merged with the firm Arbour & Wellington.
1979	– The firm opened an office in Saskatoon.
1980	– The firms adopted the names Clarkson Gordon and Woods Gordon, dropping the commas and the "& Co".
1981	– The Victoria office merged with the firm Trenholme, Winterbottom & Co.
	– The Quebec City office merged with Bélanger, Dallaire, Gagnon & Associés.
1982	– Woods Gordon celebrated its 50th anniversary.
1983	– The Newfoundland office merged with Warr, Saunders, Blackwood and Hoskins.
	– David Hooper's litigation support practice joined the Vancouver office.
	– The Saskatoon practice merged with Lacoursière & Partners.
	– The firm merged with Needham Underhill & Partners in Barrie and opened an office in that city.
1984	– Following a merger with the firm Viau, Rouleau, Brosseau & Associés, a new office was opened in Laval, Quebec.
1985	– The Clarkson Company Limited became Clarkson Gordon Inc.
1986	– The Vancouver office merged with Wilson & Co. in Richmond, opening an office in that city.

	– The Winnipeg office merged with Wirth & Wirth.
	– The York Region office opened.
	– The firm took a financial interest in Arthur Young Southeast Asia which has interests in five countries on the Pacific Rim: Hong Kong, Indonesia, Malaysia, Singapore and Thailand.
	– Clarkson Gordon took a financial interest in the Barbados firm of Arthur Young.
1987	– Walter Gordon and Duncan Gordon died.
1988	– The firm merged with Adam, Authier, Boyer et Associés, creating an office on the South Shore of Montreal.
	– The Montreal office moved to new quarters in a Montreal landmark: Place Ville Marie.
	– The Toronto office entered into a new lease arrangement to move into the new Clarkson Gordon Tower in the Toronto-Dominion Centre in 1991.
1989	– 125 years – "Committed to the future, indebted to our past."

APPENDIX II

Partners
of the Firm

As at September 1, 1988

National
P.O. Box 251,
Royal Trust Tower, T-D Centre
Toronto, Ontario M5K 1J7
Phone: (416) 864–1234
Fax: (416) 864–1174

Paul Barnicke
Gord Best
Doug Cameron
Don Cockburn
Len Delicaet
David DeWolf
Ron Ellis
Denise Esdon
Bill Farlinger
Bruce Foster
Ron Gage
Joe Gill
Tony Grant
Jean-Pierre Graveline
Mike Henderson
Don Johnston
John Kearns
John Kirkwood

David Lay
Don Leslie
Bob Lord
Fred Mallett
Barney McGrogan
Peter McKelvey
John Meek
Alex Milburn
Henry Pankratz
Ross Pearman
Murray Rumack
Bill Rupert
Terry Scandrett
David Selley
Gerry Shortall
John Swinden
Lonnie Tate
Mike Thompson
Mike Veaudry
Charlie Vincent
Peter Wood

Don Durst, Secretary Treasurer

St. John's

10 Fort William Place,
7th Floor
St. John's, Newfoundland
A1C 1K4
Phone: (709) 726–2840
Fax: (709) 726–0345

Don Blackwood
Jim Cavanagh
Bob Healey
Phil Quinlan
Don Warr

Halifax

1959 Upper Water Street,
12th Floor
Halifax, Nova Scotia B3J 2Z1
Phone: (902) 420–1080
Fax: (902) 420–0503

Paul Campbell
John Carter
Ross Landers
Carl Rumley
George Waye

Saint John

One Brunswick Square,
Suite 1209
Saint John, New Brunswick
E2L 4V1
Phone: (506) 634–7000
Fax: (506) 634–2129

Keith Bowman
John Murphy
Ron Rose
Terry Thorne

Quebec

1150, rue Claire-Fontaine,
Suite 700
Quebec, Quebec G1R 5G4
Phone: (418) 524–5151
Fax: (418) 524–0061

André Grondines
Raymond Lavoie
Jacques Levesque
Léo Linteau
Marc Mathieu
Claude Michaud

Guy Boulanger
Fernand Dufresne
Raymond Fortier
Yvon Fortin
Sheila Fraser-Gagnon

Jacques Nicole
Charles Pelletier
Benoit Racine
Noël Rhéaume
Maurice Tremblay

Montreal

1 Place Ville Marie, Suite 2400
Montreal, Quebec H3B 3M9
Phone: (514) 875–6060
Fax: (514) 871–8713

Pierre Alary
Diane Bale
Alain Benedetti
Claude Bismuth
Chuck Bissegger
Diane Blais-Ialenti
François Bolduc
Rod Budd
Tom Burpee
Cheryl Campbell Steer
Guy Chamberland
André Courville
Denis Desautels
Norm Evans
Georges Fournier
Guy Fréchette

Serge Gagné
Roger Germain
Yves Giard
Marcel Guay
Marcel Guilbault
Lucie Hétu
Denis Labrèche
Hugues Laliberté
Drummond Lamb
Michel Lanteigne
Allan Lanthier
André Laparé
Monique Leroux
Gérard Limoges
Lorraine Maheu
Richard Messier
Rudy Okker
Ron Pearl
Mike Riley
Jack Schnek
Gary Wells

Montreal South Shore

7305, boulevard Marie-Victoria
3rd Floor
Brossard, Quebec J4W 1A6
Phone: (514) 671–1960
Fax: (514) 393–1817

Pierre Adam
Jacques Authier
Serge Boyer
Arthur Pontbriand
Jacques Pontbriand

Laval

3090, boulevard Le Carrefour,
Suite 600
Laval, Quebec H7T 2J7
Phone: (514) 337–8105
Fax: (514) 337–0918

Réal Brunet
Robert Gagné
Yves Lussier
Gilles Salvas
Roland Taillefer
Michel Viau

163

Ottawa

55 Metcalfe Street, Suite 1600
Ottawa, Ontario K1P 6L5
Phone: (613) 232–1511
Fax: (613) 232–5324

Brian Barrington
Ron Batt
André Bussière
Mario Clément

Peter Cleveland
Michael Connolly
Steve Gallagher
Stu Levine
Jim Morrisey
Wayne Penny
David Roth
Alastair Sinclair

Toronto Metro-East

1200 Markham Road,
Suite 200
Scarborough, Ontario
M1H 3C3
Phone: (416) 439–8400
Fax: (416) 439–8339

Tom Abel
Jim Boyko
Ron Buckle
Brian Wallace

Toronto

P.O. Box 251,
Royal Trust Tower, T-D Centre
Toronto, Ontario M5K 1J7
Phone: (416) 864–1234
Fax: (416) 864–1174

Peter Adamson
Steve Aldersley
Ken Alles
John Anderson
Phil Arthur
Alan Backley
Roy Baldwin
Grant Beasley
Bill Beavers
Laurie Bennett

Paul Benson
Graham Bentley
Randy Billing
Richard Blanchard
Greg Boehmer
David Bolton
Richard Bradeen
Roger Briers
Denis Brown
Joe Buckley
Jim Bull
Jim Bunton
Brian Caine
John Callum
Bob Cameron
Jim Carlisle

Mike Cavanagh
Kelvin Chen
Geof Clarkson
Dan Cornacchia
Owen Crassweller
Bill Crawford
Irene David
John Davidson
Mike Denega
Barry Dent
Al Dewling
John Dickson
John Dines
David Doncaster
Bill Dunlop
Ron Dunne
Peter Farwell
Gordon Fear
Eldon Ferguson
Gus Gillespie
Tom Goldspink
Art Good
Ian Gordon
John Goudey
Colin Graham
Don Grant
Paul Gratias
Kerry Gray
John Greene
John Haag
George Hamilton
Paul Heffernan
Mo Hewitt
Nick Hodson
John Jakolev
Mike Jamani
Michael Jan

Eric Johnston
Grant Jones
Ron Knechtel
Ken Laundy
Rick Lemon
Colin Lipson
David Little
Pete Little
Bob Long
Rollie Lutes
Terry Marlow
Fraser Mason
Phil Matthews
Mike McClew
Jack McGregor
Henry McKinlay
Rob McLean
Colleen McMorrow
Gerry McMunn
Lou Meehan
Owen Menzel
Paul Michaelis
Bob Mitchell
Leigh Morris
Lynda Mungall
Ken Musgrave
Aldo Neim
Mark O'Regan
Eric Ostfield
Ron Peters
John Playfair
Lloyd Posno
Harold Reiter
David Richardson
David Rittenhouse
Fred Ritzmann
Paul Roberts

Toronto (cont'd)

Nick Ross
Walter Ross
Barry Rowland
Al Russell
Morris Schnek
Ron Scott
Steve Shaver
Paul Singleton
Ron Smith
Roy Steel
Hap Stephen
Barb Stymiest
Stu Sutcliffe
Bob Sutherland
Tibor Szandtner
Steve Tanny
Sheryl Teed

Martha Tory
Bob Turner
Bill Vanderburgh
Steve Wace
Bruce Ward
Peter Watkins
Charlie Webster
Karen Wensley
Linda Willis
Mike Wills
Fraser Wilson
John Wilson
Mike Wood
Mark Woodruff
Mike Wright
David Yule

Barrie

85 Bayfield Street, Suite 401
Barrie, Ontario L4M 3A7
Phone: (705) 728–3397
Fax: (705) 728–2728

Tom Hards
Charles Jeffery
Gary Pearson
Bryan Underhill

Mississauga

201 City Centre Drive,
Suite 705
Mississauga, Ontario L5B 2T4
Phone: (416) 270–2121
Fax: (416) 270–9984

Bruce Barraclough
John Blodgett
Ron Bogart

Mike Doucher
Anne Edgar
David Leslie
Jim Lutes
Bill McDermott
Dave Pollard
Doug Smith
Dave Stephen

York Region
300 John Street, Suite 602
Thornhill, Ontario L3T 5W4
Phone: (416) 731-1500
Fax: (416) 731-1500 (x. 233)

Don Gillespie
Peter Mashinter
Jim Rayside
Jack Taylor
Garry West

Hamilton
100 King Street West,
4th Floor
Hamilton, Ontario L8P 1A2
Phone: (416) 526-8880
Fax: (416) 526-9935

Eric Anderson
Murray Halpren

David Hector
Paul Jaggard
Bob Neale
Barry Nicol
Brooke Townsend
Ted Urbanowicz
Bill Willson

Kitchener
305 King Street West,
9th Floor
Kitchener, Ontario N2G 4A2
Phone: (519) 744-1171
Fax: (519) 744-9604

Bob Blowes
Rod Cleaver
John Cowperthwaite

Bill Goss
Howie Jasper
Terry Lalande
Randy Martin
Doug Montgomery
Dick Pedlar
Gary Pooley
Terry Reidel

London
City Centre
380 Wellington Street,
London, Ontario N6A 5B5
Phone: (519) 672-6100
Fax: (519) 438-5785

Bruce Beckett

Zbig Biskup
Tom Boone
Wes Douglas
Ed Heslin
Denis Lemieux
Brian Lessard

London (cont'd)

Doug McDonald
Pat McGrath
John Morris
Barrie Neal
Al Owen
John Porter

David Preston
John Reed
Osama Sherif
John Stein
Bill Stuart
Bill Wood

Windsor

374 Ouellette Avenue,
Suite 700
Windsor, Ontario N9A 6W4
Phone: (519) 255–1211
Fax: (519) 255–9846

Bill Carter
Jim Macri
Tony Mancinone
Vic Neufeld

Thunder Bay

215 Red River Road, Suite 200
Thunder Bay, Ontario P7B 5J9
Phone: (807) 343–5400
Fax: (807) 345–8314

Glenn Brassard
Ken Bruley
Bob Geddes

Winnipeg

360 Main Street, Suite 2700
Winnipeg, Manitoba R3C 4G9
Phone: (204) 947–6519
Fax: (204) 956–0138

Jim Bryce
Gus Campbell
Peter Dueck
Mike Evans

Dan Kraayeveld
Gordon Law
Al Moore
Dave Morison
Ralph Palmer
Denis Posten
Don Price
Gavin Todd
John Wirth

Regina

2103 – 11th Avenue, Suite 900
Regina, Saskatchewan S4P 3Z8
Phone: (306) 569–1234
Fax: (306) 757–4753

Joe Anton
Dennis Gray

Doug Johnson
Ed Kendrick
Archie Ledgerwood
Peter Stephen
David Thompson
Bob Watt
Gord Wicijowski

Saskatoon

219 Robin Crescent, Suite 200
Saskatoon, Saskatchewan
S7L 6M8
Phone: (306) 652–6594
Fax: (306) 653–1553

Shelley Brown
Bob Henderson
Bob Lacoursiere
Ray Taylor

Calgary

707 – 7th Avenue S.W.,
Suite 1300
Calgary, Alberta T2P 3H6
Phone: (403) 290–4100
Fax: (403) 290–4265

Bill Best
Glen Braum
Wayne Brock
Dave Connolly
Glen Cronkwright
Vick Dusik
David Finlay
Gordon Forbes
Sandy Grant
Ron Isaac
Rick Lancaster

Peter Lane
Graham LeBourveau
Chris LeGeyt
Guy Levy
John Lowden
Barney McCoshen
Eric Morgan
Ian Robinson
Greg Rodych
John Rouse
Steve Slipp
Crawford Smith
Fred Snell
John Stankiewicz
Don Stewart
Ian Sutherland

Edmonton

10060 Jasper Avenue,
Suite 1800, Esso Tower
Edmonton, Alberta T5J 3R8
Phone: (403) 423–5811
Fax: (403) 428–8977

Mike Andrews
Chuck Austin
Gordon Barefoot

Rick Cormier
Glen Heximer
Russ Law
Andre Lemieux
Bob McColl
Jack McMahon
Ian Strang
Les Tutty

Vancouver

700 West Georgia Street
Vancouver, British Columbia
V7Y 1C7
Phone: (604) 683–7133
Fax: (604) 643–5422

Ian Adam
Michael Adams
Ken Cross
Bill Drake
Doug Eakins
Clark Gallon
David Hooper

John Hutton
Ken Ingo
Terry Jonat
John Kuss
Bonar Lund
Rob Mackay
Neil MacKenzie
Larry Prentice
David Rickards
Heather Shannon
Jim Stuart
Tom Wall
Fred Withers

Richmond

10711 Cambie Road, Suite 206
Richmond, British Columbia
V6X 3G5
Phone: (604) 276–0759
Fax: (604) 276–0521

Dennis Bettiol
Alan Lazzari
Larry Phillips
Craig Wilson

Victoria
1175 Douglas Street,
Suite 1010
Victoria, British Columbia
V8W 2V3
Phone: (604) 386–3521
Fax: (604) 386–8488

Brian Dyer
Vern Fitzgerald
Stan Haughey
John Heraghty

TYPESETTING
University of Toronto Press

PRINTING
University of Toronto Press

PAPER
Miami Book 110M

BINDING MATERIAL
Columbia Milbank Linen

BINDING
T.H. Best

DESIGN
William Rueter RCA